Edith Henderson's
HOME
LANDSCAPE
Companion

Edith Henderson's HOME LANDSCAPE Companion

Edith Henderson

Illustrated by
VICKY HOLIFIELD

PEACHTREE PUBLISHERS, LTD.
Atlanta

Published by

PEACHTREE PUBLISHERS, LTD.

494 Armour Circle, NE
Atlanta, Georgia 30324

Text © 1993 Edith Henderson
Illustrations © 1993 Vicky Holifield

Jacket design by Candace J. Magee

Composition by Twin Studios, Atlanta

Manufactured in the United States of America

10 9 8 7 6 5 4 3 2 1

Library of Congress Cataloging-in-Publication Data

Henderson, Edith, 1911-
   [Home landscape companion]
   Edith Henderson's home landscape companion /
Edith Henderson; illustrated by Vicky Holifield.
     p.   cm.
   Includes index.
   ISBN 1-56145-079-0
   1. Landscape design. 2. Landscape gardening. I. Title.
II. Title: Home landscape companion.
SB473.H43 1993
93-8552
712′ .6--dc20   93-8552
                                               CIP

Jacket illustration: Detail from "The Sunny South,"
George Woltze (attr.), c. 1889. Oil on canvas. Property of
Morris Museum of Art, Augusta, Georgia

Dedication

This book is dedicated to the memory of Edith Daniel and Charles Edward Harrison, my mother and father. During our lives together, they fulfilled many a wish with love and understanding. They quickly realized my fascination with anything growing, and through the years they turned me in the right direction to follow my longing to create beauty everywhere.

A very special heartfelt "thank you" goes to James Ross Henderson, Sr., my husband of more than fifty years. He took my hand in his and has always walked with me along this path that we both love. He, too, is a close friend of all growing things.

Edith Henderson

CONTENTS

A Note to the Reader

I cannot imagine any career being more satisfying than mine as a landscape architect. Whether I am working with an owner or a tenant of a plot of ground, a home, a large estate, or a condominium, I am always excited by the challenge and gratified by any beauty I can help to create.

With licenses in six states and reciprocity in others, I have enjoyed practicing in all of the major fields of my profession over a great part of the United States. I soon realized that, wherever and whatever the project, my consultation with the client did not have to be a long, complicated affair involving a formal report. Two hours on a site was generally all that was necessary.

I developed a technique of making detailed sketches and notes as I surveyed the property. At the end of my visit, I turned these over to my client. Using this neat and workable process, I was providing a basic "design plan" that could be implemented all at once or step by step by the energetic do-it-yourselfer, or with professional landscaping assistance as needed.

When I wrote a weekly newspaper column later in my career, I found that I was able to describe landscape design concepts that readers could grasp. They could use my words to make their surroundings more livable and pleasant every day of the year.

Now I am writing this book so that I can walk with you and give you landscape design ideas for the starkness of winter—when nature is bared to the bone and you should do your planning—as well as for the outburst of spring, the fecundity of summer, and the mellow golden season of fall. From my own lifetime partnership with nature, I want to tell my secrets for protecting and enjoying all of the growing things with which we have been blessed.

Keep these secrets close by and your own lifetime partnership will have begun.

How to Use This Book

Behold! A list of everything you ever wanted to tackle around your house and in your garden.

This book is organized by the seasons, beginning with winter. Then month by month, spring, summer, and fall follow in their natural order. The design and horticultural ideas are matched to the rhythm of nature, though many of them may be considered any time of the year.

I start with winter because everything is exposed and visible. This is the perfect time to see your property in its bleakest phase, down to its barest structure. The basic design is before your eyes. You can see how all of the elements such as walks, walls, fences, statuary, pools, and the arrangements of trees, shrubs, and flower beds are related to each other. Begin to see what you have, and you can begin putting together your design plan.

I shall tell you how to create a design plan, but the content of *your own* plan will evolve gradually as you become more aware of how the features of your yard and house (or a church garden or commercial setting—whatever your specific project) work together, or do not work together. My book will be your companion; it will explain the principles of design and how you can apply them. These are practical, sensible rules that you can put to work, experiment with, and modify. Allow yourself this experience of changing, discarding, and adding in the planning process until you are rewarded with more beautiful results than you have ever dreamed of.

Take a slow walk around your property with an inexpensive, spiral-bound notebook and pencil in hand. Start with simple sketches and notes about things as they are. Remember, this notebook is for you; don't worry about how artistic your sketches are. Get down the general "lay of the land" from different vantage points and notes about what is growing on it. In later drawings you can incorporate more details and actual measurements.

You might begin at the front of your property, sitting on a stool or a portable lawn chair, near the street. Observe, sketch, make some notes; then move to the side yards and the back, ending up at your rear property line.

Quite a trip, and quite a few notes. This may be the first time that you have actually concentrated on property lines—the back, the front, both sides.

Begin to pay attention to your own yard and to the landscapes all around you. You will become more conscious of the uses of color and texture; you will see patterns and relationships, proportion and balance, with fresh eyes. This experience is a process, but most of all it is an adventure. Use this book as the guide for your adventure.

The horticultural information in this book refers most closely to the states of the mid-Atlantic through the lower south from the east coast to parts of the southwest and even up into the northwest (zones 6,7, and 8 of the Plant Hardiness Zone Map published by the U.S. Department of Agriculture). Readers in other areas of this country or from other countries can easily substitute plant suggestions and seasonal information better suited to their local conditions.

The design information, of course, is not limited to any particular locale.

Introduction

In the south we are surrounded by a rich heritage of horticultural knowledge and design information. It is wise to go slowly and step lightly while learning how to use it. The wonder of holding living plant material in your hand and having a clear picture of what to do with it in your head must be tempered by understanding the value of a comprehensive design plan. Creating a plan on paper, detail by detail, is essential if you are going to bring all of the elements of your property into harmony and create the effect that you want.

No matter how high you may fly in creating beautiful surroundings, stay in touch with reality. It is much easier to erase an unworkable part of a plan on paper, or make a new sketch, than it is to shift actual plants to more acceptable locations. So, we know from the beginning that a plan is the agreement you have with the plant material, the seasons, and the available space.

In this agreement there is a reminder that muted colors are gentle, brilliant colors assertive, and that both prefer being planted in groups of their own kind, never alternated. Hold fast to a chosen color, feel the textures, keep the design clear of unnecessary extras, and your plan will continue to live and breathe with you.

There should be a tendency to feel humble when in the presence of any growing thing. No matter how many hours you watch, rarely will you be able to see that vine reach up and attach itself to an overhead wire or observe a daisy turning to face the sun. But, they do it in their own way.

Learning to understand the entire process is the first step toward beginning to design a place for plants to live, to be happy, and to prosper. The polite procedure is to think through what you expect them to do, then try the idea out on a few plants. The *idea* is enough at first, and only then is it time to draw up a basic plan.

In choosing plants for designated areas in your design plan, follow a few simple rules. Place the plants in locations where they will get the amount of sun or shade they will need. Don't forget that some plants prefer shade. Use enough of one plant to show off its personality. Plant all material in stairsteps: low to medium to high. Don't jump around. Avoid mixing thorny plants with smooth, gentle varieties. More about the basic rules of design as we go along.

The amount of space from the front of the house to the street is of great importance. Many otherwise attractive houses seem to tilt toward the street. If you are building, there is a rule of thumb to follow. Calculate the height of the front of the house from the top ridgepole of the roof to the ground. There should be at least that much distance from the bottom of your front steps to the street. If your house is on a deep lot, just be sure to abide by this rule, then changes in width and grades only add interest to the overall plan.

Begin at the street and walk toward the house. Can you see it? You should see at least a corner or a window, or else there may be the disorienting feeling that you are at the back instead of the front.

The front walk should enhance the beauty of the house and be welcoming to guests. It should be a minimum of four feet wide and absolutely smooth, and its pattern should be a delight to the eye. Do not trap a person on the walk by thick planting on both sides. Children are apt to try to jump such borders, a snake can hide under them, and there is that urge to walk through them.

Rub the bark of a nearby tree, touch the deeply serrated leaves of a vine, smell the roses and pansies, and know that the miracle of close friendship with nature has just begun.

With our natural wealth of plant material, there is great seasonal beauty for the seeing and fruit for the eating. Ample shade trees produce unbelievable fall beauty. Evergreen trees and shrubs are escorts through winter months and backgrounds for all spring blooming plants. Flowering shrubs, trees, ground covers, annuals, and perennials unfailingly announce the arrival of spring and summer.
The gifts of the seasons are almost overwhelming, but be restrained in your response. You could, for instance, prune plant material into bright yellow or purple balls. Better to hold back until you understand what nature is trying to accomplish. Remember that you are not really in charge.

Resist the flamboyant plant on sale unless it would be happy with the surrounding healthy plants and unless it fits into your design. Let us begin now to gather together thoughts, words, colors, and shapes as we create a comprehensive plan that will bring into harmony all of the elements in your particular piece of earth.

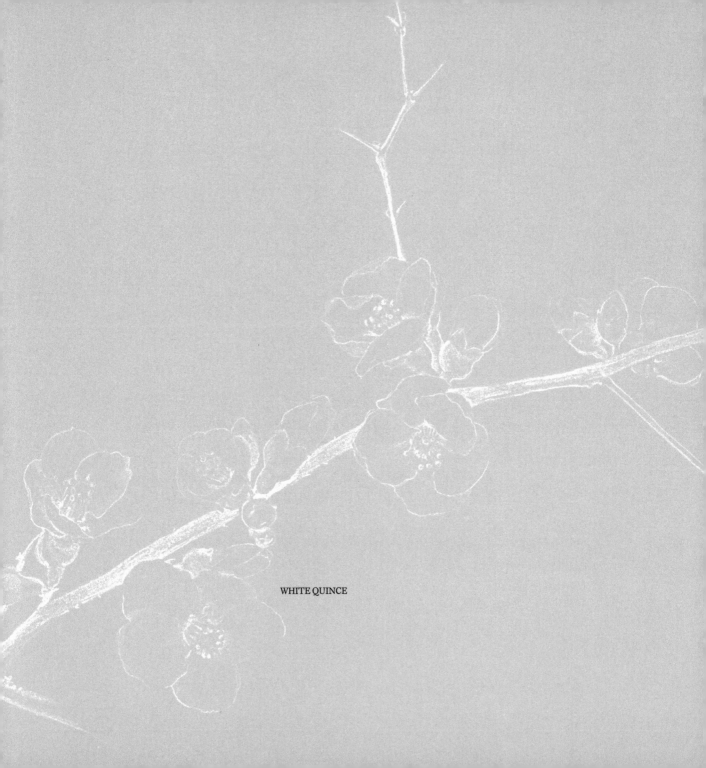

WHITE QUINCE

Winter

December · January · February

In winter months we are setting the stage for the living, fascinating show we shall see in spring. Whatever you have planned, such as shrub grouping, the position of trees, green areas, and color massing of flowers, all will be most beautiful in March, April, and May. But do not forget the dramatic possibilities for winter.

Become more familiar with the many varieties of broadleaf evergreens, especially the dwarfs. These low-profile shrubs are always needed to spray over and out of planter boxes, to soften flights of steps, and to break up sharp lines of long, low garden walls. Boxleaf holly, the twelve-inch *Ilex helleri,* dwarf yaupon holly, dwarf gardenia, and cotoneaster—each creates an admirable effect.

A word about plant suggestions: As we go along, I shall offer examples of appropriate plants. Some may be familiar, but do not worry if they are not. If you are just beginning to learn about plants, you will want to browse through your local nursery selections, nursery catalogs, and some of the many excellent books that picture and identify plants. Gardening enthusiasts enjoy talking about their subject, and you will find as much help as you decide you need from the staff at any good nursery, county extension agents, and the landscape professionals in your area.

Part of winter planning is correcting old mistakes. Do something, for example, about the azalea groups that turned out to be the wrong color. Remember that best results are always obtained, especially in small areas, by planting one color only. A mixture of colors is tiring and usually not successful. If there is room to introduce another tone in, say, a twenty-five-foot space, go ahead, but be conservative.

Any bulbs, such as tulips, hyacinths, and scillas, need a uniform background. A conglomeration of high and low shrubs or two kinds of adjoining fences do not help the picture at all. Clipped green boxleaf holly or weathered wood fencing will give cool, lovely results. The scillas are forever, and only tulips need renewing about every third year.

When planning shrubs and trees, think not only of the best varieties but also of size. At the top of your list of plants for immediate or future purchase, write, **You get what you pay for!** Underline it with red ink. So-called trees that look like switches, and shrubs that resemble a group of sticks will get you nowhere very fast. Even the bargain price is wasted money.

As you place the shrubs, remember that often no continuous line is needed. Bands of evergreen ground cover such as dwarf mondo and regular and dwarf ivy serve beautifully to connect one group of shrubs to another.

Open spaces are immediately evident in winter. Some open area is necessary if you are going to emphasize a focal point such as a perfectly shaped evergreen tree or a piece of statuary. The focal point is used as a visual device to organize the way a viewer sees the landscape. Other spaces might serve as foregrounds for gardens framed in evergreen hedges, for fences covered with miniature ivy or evergreen Carolina yellow jessamine. We are working toward an effect that has beauty and balance, not a blast of color.

Give the simplest little house enough space for beautifully, tastefully balanced planting and it will resemble a small palace. But fill the same lot with an unappealing

PITTOSPORUM

mix of plants, narrow walkways, uneven stepping stones, dirt paths, narrow steps, or a driveway wrapped around the house, and simple beauty and serenity are gone.

Winter is study and planning time, so take courage in hand and look at all sides of your lot, especially if it is long and narrow. Too often, there is bumpy, unattractive grading. One side of the lot may resemble a cliff, while the other side might be fairly level. Walls can enhance the overall beauty of the entire lot when used to raise grades to the same level or to make transitions between grades.

If your house has a southern or western exposure, this would be an exceptionally fine spot for a rose garden or flower border. An entire side may be shady, just the place to plant funkia (hosta), *Torenia,* bleeding heart, caladium, begonia, lily of the valley, aucuba, mahonia, or leucothoe. Evergreen ground cover is another choice, or you could lay stepping stones or fine pea gravel, with a planting area on the outer edge for a balanced, easy walk. Keep in mind that there is not just one correct way to treat an area. Your design plan can and should reflect your individual taste and desires, and your expanding knowledge of good design principles.

Tight spots, if handled well, are very often the most attractive part of the landscape because the limitation of space forces you to locate each plant for its own best effect. Detailed beauty in small spaces can mean more than a magnificent fifty-foot flower border.

Wouldn't it be a delight to get a jump on that neglected outdoor sitting area before the weather turns warm? While checking on necessary spaces for tables and chairs, note existing plantings and start designing an overhaul. Almost anything can be grown in a tub or pot, so don't let lack of planting space stop you. Mahonia, aucuba, and loropetalum will take care of shady areas easily. They can be started in containers, kept in a sheltered place for winter, and placed as needed in spring. It will be a delight to sit close to fragrant plants later, especially if they include a few standard gardenias. Then there are handsome photinias and dwarf Burford hollies, which always seem to be at their best.

Do not allot too much space to materials that bloom before you can enjoy the terrace or other outdoor space. Instead of early azaleas, plant indica and tall and dwarf macrantha azaleas. In place of too many tulips, plant begonias, green-and-white hosta, primroses, amaryllis, and dwarf and tall marigolds after the frost. Redbud trees are fine for terrace shade, but you might miss their bloom completely as it is usually too chilly to sit outside when they are in flower. So, plant dogwoods or flowering cherries instead, which bloom a bit later.

A sound investment is to plant handsome green shrubs close by for year-round beauty. Consider variegated green-and-white holly (which can be hard to find) or camellias—white-blooming ones trained as vines on any kind of wall or groups of pink camellias in semishade—anise and pittosporum, English holly, and not one abelia! Nearby, place a Carolina hemlock and a corner planting of large, fat loquats with weeping ligustrums around their feet. If there is a really conspicuous, ugly detail of some sort, look for the richest evergreen tree you can find, such as a Nellie Stevens holly. Plant a group of three of these large shrubs that actually grow into trees, and the problem will disappear.

Plan now for a special place to locate a *Chionanthus virginica* (fringe tree or grancy graybeard). It is so beautiful when covered with fragrant white clusters of flowers that it might be a splendid idea to give a party in its honor at the height of its bloom (April in the lower South and May in the upper South). Male fringe trees are the showiest; yet, female trees produce clusters of blue, olive-like fruit that hang in panicles in late summer and are very special to all types of birds.

Take time to be sure of all details, and the winter months will be your evergreen bridge to a beautiful spring.

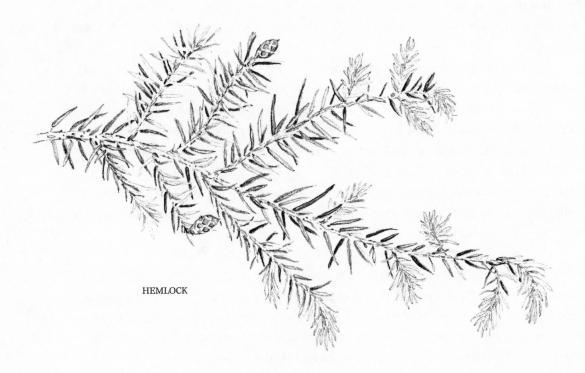

HEMLOCK

DECEMBER

Stretch Your Imagination

Land forms are a fascinating study. As a matter of fact, if they were studied more and changed less, our surroundings would be more inspiring.

Many tree problems are caused by drastic land changes that upset water tables and cause trees to go into shock. Before developing any land, it would be a great thing if the owner would say, "Now, what have we here? How can I handle this land to the best possible *natural* advantage?"

Study of the land should permeate every phase of outdoor design. Successful design of homes, schools, churches, apartments, stores, walkways, streets, freeways, parks—every area in which people live and move—depends on understanding the use of land forms close around us. If we are sensitive to the land, we can manage other problems as they arise.

Working on one's own lot is about the most intimate relationship a person can have with a piece of land. So, as background, try to find out what your land was like before you and your house (or church or business) arrived. Existing trees are a good lead; if they are all on original grade and are developing well, no doubt your house is well placed and presents a pleasing composition.

Where the grade level around trees has been raised, you can see, or soon will be able to, that the trees are slowly dying. The entire area has been traumatized, and there is trouble ahead. For every important tree, plan to locate a seedling of the same variety, or a suitable substitute if you prefer, and place it near the existing tree. This will assure in the future the leafy setting that the lot had originally.

If you have healthy native plant material on the lot, consider yourself lucky. This material not only saves you time and money, but also provides outdoor compositions with growth that is unlikely to freeze or die. Look twice at fine groups of existing sumac, sassafras, ferns, huckleberry, and hawthorn. You have the basic elements to create a stunning effect.

A Thoughtful Use of Winter Space

One of the most valuable contributions of a design plan can be a thoughtful strategy for the use of uncluttered, unadorned space. When the space is vast, a few trees standing alone can be as perfect as a stage setting. White oaks and sugar maples, low-branching pines, black gums, pink weeping crabapples, weeping willows, silverbell trees, and sourwoods immediately come into their own. They are superb winter silhouettes.

A feeling of space means much more in winter, especially when evergreen trees and ample shrubs are part of the design. Some open areas can be completely satisfying as rolling, grassy lawns; others can be more attractive as fields. There is no pressing upkeep problem with fields, which need to be mowed or sickled only two or three times a year.

Where fields are left, brilliant patches of color spring up among rough grasses as various types of annual wildflower seeds naturalize. Among adaptable kinds are the showy evening primrose, mixed four o'clocks, annual phlox, annual mixed *Gaillardia,* balsam for shady sections, larkspur, crotolaria, cornflower, and double Shirley poppy, all of which reseed themselves.

That small wild meadow beyond the lawn can become quite a sight with combined masses of blue cornflowers and yellow poppies or pink larkspur or pink-and-white annual phlox. To keep the bloom thick and to ensure plentiful growth year after year, scatter extra seeds at the time when plants are naturally dropping them.

When space is a scarce commodity, the thoughtful use of it is like a breath of fresh air. We need it badly in cities, in small towns, and in our own backyards. It is a definite asset around many office buildings and should be jealously guarded. When a great area is laid out before our eyes for our enjoyment, we instantly realize how cluttered most spaces have become. Uncluttered space is a priceless possession that will not be with us long unless we protect it.

Wide open spaces as seen in winter are often exactly the right setting for masses of flowering shrubs. Begin by locating a large mass of one variety of plant. Do not mix varieties in the same group.

Now is your chance to cut back arborvitaes and cedars if they are growing against a building as foundation plants. If you prune now, missing limbs and foliage will not even be noticed during the summer. Remember, the trees you prune need never again be allowed to get too tall or too wide.

Simplify all late winter work by opening up ob congested spaces and letting a little breeze blow thro Do some checking on the locations of existing trees. Are there too many in one location and not enough in another? Careful pruning can create one miracle, and the use of evergreen ground covers under and around trees can create another. Dwarf mondo plays an important role here: no cutting, no upkeep except water, easy on the feet, grows in sun or shade

DWARF MONDO

JANUARY

Bone Structure

January is the truthful month. The bone structure of every outdoor area is totally revealed as weak or strong. Either there is obvious balance, or it is clear that the area has fallen apart. If the latter is true, spend a little time planning backgrounds of broadleaf evergreen material or evergreen enclosures of walls or fences. The design can be very simple. Groups of dwarf holly and aucuba in flower beds along with annuals and perennials will keep your design in place regardless of weather and the calendar.

If the focal point of a large space happens to be a swimming pool, plant clusters of evergreen trees nearby to insure that there will be some shade year-round. Carolina hemlock, dwarf magnolia, and holly not only produce shade but also present an amazing contrast in evergreen foliage.

When deciduous trees lose their leaves they become immediate silhouettes, and some suffer by comparison. For instance, a paulownia or a mimosa is never stunning in silhouette, but beeches, maples, sourwoods, white oaks, and many others provide a handsome show all winter long. The cold months can be times of great beauty.

Think flowers in winter, too. Plant daffodils now among clumps of trees. Plant them in great masses according to color—the Mount Hood, Duke of Windsor, Golden Harvest, Thalia. Plant hyacinths in large groups, but never in straight lines!

Remember that the best kind of gardening always recognizes the value of existing material but has the ability to take on new varieties with great aplomb. This adaptability helps keep your design plan different and fresh.

Lay down a few simple rules to follow—even if there are days when you are not about to follow any of them! Be careful to note on your design plan the plants that must have sun and those that prefer a touch of shade. Constantly remind yourself that muted colors are gentle, easy companions; brilliant colors are assertive. And both prefer to be planted in groups of their own kind, never alternated. Keep your design clear of unnecessary "volunteer" plants, and those you want will continue to live and breathe as planned.

The Useful Design Plan

From the beginning, a design plan is central. It can help you solve existing problems and avoid new ones. So, before changing any plant material, go across the street and take a long, slow look at your house and lot. Then, walk all the way around your property. Startling, isn't it?

You are likely to discover some very attractive spots, but then you may see some unconnected areas with no particular reason for being. The latter may contain carefully chosen shrubs and trees that look good individually, but each one appears to be totally on its own, not blending with its background.

Now is the time to go to work. It takes patience and courage to get out the notebook and pencil, but do just that. Sit down at the front of your property and begin.

Sketch in, however roughly, your house and every flower bed, shrub, tree, and vine. Add all the features: driveway, sidewalks, any walls, even the mailbox.

The first result of your sketching will be a new awareness of how the world around you looks. There may be groups of fine, sturdy shrubs and trees, but do members of a group accept each other? Or, are there singles all over the place,

Sketch in, however roughly, your house and every flower bed, shrub, tree, and vine.

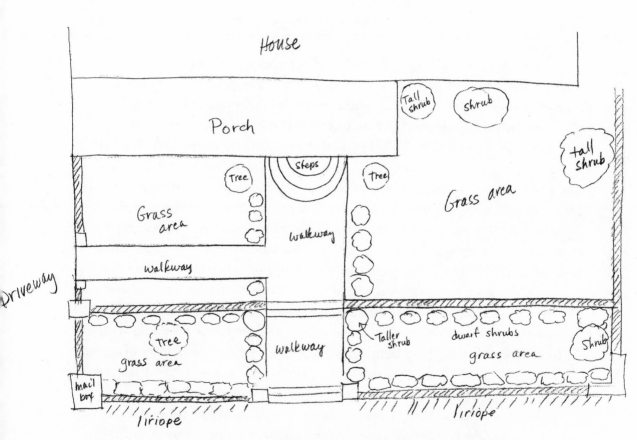

Add all the features: driveway, sidewalks, any walls, even the mailbox.

perhaps even pruned in different ways, that seem lonesome? The appearance of your lot may be unsatisfactory for several reasons. You can see that some plants are happy together, and others will never like the company that has been forced upon them.

Different plants have different personalities. For instance, plants with sharply pointed leaves jammed against plants with smooth, delicate foliage will never blend. So, not being congenial, they seem restless and limp. But, give the smooth ones a space of their own to breathe and grow, and prickly ones their own corner, and all will be content.

Break the habit of lining up everything; lines of plants are unnatural and monotonous. Instead, plan to place like varieties together in groups of three or more with breathing spaces between groups, creating patterns of richness and diversity.

Be aware of the importance of backgrounds in design. Picture totally different plants such as red- or yellow-fruited pyracantha or white-flowering camellias introduced as backgrounds for dwarf evergreen boxwoods and dwarf holly. The possibilities for stunning compositions are endless. Remember, also, the dwarf azaleas with an ultimate height of eighteen inches and dwarf variegated green-and-white hollies that grow to about thirty inches. If space permits, add versatile evergreen trees ranging from stately dwarf magnolias (twelve to fifteen feet) to medium hollies such as *Ilex pernyi* at twenty feet to perfect hemlocks stretching upward to fifty and sixty feet.

If there are too many varieties of trees on the property, the lot is bound to resemble a nursery. Instead, you want stunning panoramas of richness in shapes, textures, and colors, in berry and bloom. So, plan slowly by grouping trees according to variety. Three different varieties planted in a group will surely pull any semblance of a design totally apart and will create restlessness in other parts of your developing plan. Be thoughtful in grouping, and prevent future problems by solving existing ones.

While we are considering major elements of the design plan, study areas that are set aside for grass, including space for play and for walking. There are different mixtures of grass seed that will handle all special requirements—some producing a thick, hardy carpet and some providing a more delicate, fragile grass. Here again, you can get any needed assistance from your local nursery and other landscaping professionals as well as from reference books.

Proper maintenance of plant materials is another subject you will want to become familiar with as you make decisions about your design plan. Prune with care, but do prune, keeping in mind a plant's natural shape. The inappropriate use of unnatural ball or spike shapes will not create a pleasing effect. Although there may be space for plant material in many different natural shapes, it is always best to plan ahead for ultimate heights by pruning lightly along the way.

Feeding is as necessary to all growing things as sunshine and shade. Be sure to use a rich grade of fertilizer on trees, shrubs, vines, and climbing or bush roses—and read the directions first.

Since January is the dormant season for most shrubs and perennials, any can be moved if necessary. Sow seeds now of sweet peas, larkspur, and cornflowers, and watch their strong, steady growth.

It is important that "unnecessary extras" be eliminated from a design plan. Deciding just what is unnecessary is, of course, a very personal judgment. Though from time to time there may be something whimsical you wish to enjoy, it is good advice to avoid "cute" items that are uncongenial with the natural setting.

Go slowly and let nature be your guide. As you observe and learn more about design and horticulture, you will begin to sense the best use of the material you are working with in your piece of earth.

FEBRUARY

Nature Is Changing Its Dress

Spring is surely coming, but before it arrives pull up a chair and take another long look at house and lot. Winter is rough. One day birds sing, bulbs sprout, and the next day we have snow. Then along comes a stiff, frigid wind that sweeps everything loose into a great pile. The elements play havoc with terrace, gardens, walks, and woods, and the only way to counteract them is to have a steady, well-executed design plan in place.

Regardless of weather, a carefully designed landscape will remain in fine shape, especially when framed in excellent stone, brick, and wood. Leaves and weeds will collect, of course, but the work that represents a good idea prevails. Even through snow and rain, there should be quite a fine effect visible—brick steps outlined by their wrought-iron railing, leading to the carefully chosen feature that stands before a curtain of evergreens. Weather does not destroy such fine details, nor does it mar handsome benches, well-proportioned entrance posts, or colorful backgrounds of pruned hedges of holly or barberry. Hedges, by the way, need not always be straight; they can curve in graceful arcs or follow a free-form line dividing one space from another.

The extra time spent in thinking through combinations of textures and colors of brick, stone, wood, and concrete pays off handsomely when materials are true to a workable idea and nothing slips. The basic principle: Each segment of the design must blend into the next.

Steps and walkways should keep going until their goals are reached. They should not stop suddenly because the grade has completed its rise or fall. Be sure to connect all parts of the property logically. Isolated bits are a waste of time and effort, and in winter they are apt simply to disappear.

With nothing hidden now out-of-doors, it is fairly simple to list priorities. The first is usually privacy, a coveted element in all seasons. Another priority—and one of life's greatest pleasures at this time of year—is the planning of cut-flower and vegetable beds for heavy yield and light maintenance. The first requirements are that they be planned and protected. One of the best protections for such an area is to encircle it with a wire fence embedded in an evergreen hedge.

This austere month is also the time to dwell upon delightful subjects such as focal points. From different vantage points—inside and outside the house—notice where your eye is drawn to rest. Where do elements of the yard converge? Experiment with alternate spots. When you have identified a strong focal point, look with an unusually critical eye to see how it works with the setting of the entire house.

Low outlines of dwarf Burford holly, medium backgrounds of sheared podocarpus, and high hedges of clipped cherry laurel provide stunning frames to different areas, which may feature a bench, a jet of water, or a statue as their focal points. No focal point should be without the help of evergreen material at any time of the year. Even in winter, you can create a great effect with evergreen groups that do exactly what they should do in framing outdoor compositions, and tree groups that are well balanced and handsome.

Mark trees and shrubs that are obviously unnecessary and can be removed. Note useless stepping-stone paths and that bare fence corner, which, if it is to remain, must have a mass of color throughout all seasons. Plan ahead to make it striking with the use of such brilliant blooming plants as marigolds and tritomas. Blessed is the house that has no horrifying winter revelations, that holds in steady balance with a rich green overlay.

Winter Patterns

Winter designs are the choice extras available to everyone. If you have the time and the patience to create swirls and swags, squares and ovals, diamonds and masses of evergreens, you will be richly rewarded. There will be a feast for the eyes in green, silver-gray, yellow-green, or bronze-green plant material. You will add months of warmth and beauty to the garden world that otherwise might remain a monotone in gray.

Do a little experimenting with a simple fleur-de-lis or an extended *S* curve, and notice how clear-cut and uncluttered it appears in the midst of winter. Entire borders of evergreen ground covers planted in overlapping shell designs can warm every month with color.

Evergreen designs of dwarf yaupon holly, arranged in beds with thick mats of pine straw, are at their best between November and April. A bed's outline might be a dwarf liriope that begins and ends with *Pachysandra* ovals. Between both ends of the *Pachysandra* ovals, picture bronze *Ajuga* followed by variegated *Pachysandra*, white-flowering *Vinca minor*, small English ivy, *Sarcococca*, and *Euonymus coloratus*.

BURFORD
HOLLY

You can keep any background wall from seeming too high, too rugged, or too plain with fine espaliers or trained vines. The creative use of ivy trained in swags on the surfaces of gray walls always gives the impression of having just been hung there for a very festive occasion. These designs of deep green, well done and carefully tended, are for always.

Gray days and intense cold emphasize the beauty and value of evergreens. They create an air of warmth and luxury even in the absence of color in the surrounding landscape.

Any evergreen is far more interesting when you see it in contrast with other evergreens with different kinds of foliage. Evergreen barberry or yaupon holly enhances the beauty of the *Camellia japonica's* foliage when they are in contrast. Guava and cleyera present colorful groups of silver gray-green and velvet-green with rose pink overcasts; podocarpus acts as a dark green curtain behind azaleas of lighter green.

The large holly family possesses all sizes and shapes and colors of foliage. Without bringing in any other kind of plant, it is possible to combine many tones and textures for a most interesting planting composition. Choices begin with smooth-leaf Burfords and end with prickly-leaved *Ilex pernyi.*

ILEX PERNYI

Mid-winter teaches us valuable lessons concerning the use of stunning evergreen trees. One hemlock is a feast for the eyes, but, where space permits, groups of them are even more beautiful. One anise *(Illicium)* is a delightful accent, and several create rich, full masses of luxuriant green.

At this time of year plants stand very much alone unless grouped carefully. If plants are used to create a hedge, they will give an extremely weak effect unless planted close enough to form a continuous, unbroken line. There should be no gaps in hedges.

BARBERRY

Careful pruning goes a long way in shaping broadleaf evergreen material as it grows. Cherry laurel plants of many sizes can be coaxed into a natural conformity by patient clipping during their first year. Nandina responds very well to hard pruning, but the story is different when handling "needle-like" material such as Pfitzer junipers; they insist upon remaining complete individuals, reminding us from the beginning that they would rather take care of themselves.

Magnolias and cherry laurel trees are especially valuable, lifting their rich, dark-green foliage from the ground to amazing heights. Notice the difference a background of such choice evergreen groups makes as winter slips through the door, leaving center stage for spring.

Remember that this odds-and-ends month of February is tired, and the out-of-doors is apt to look ragged. Evergreens are February's backbone. They shake off the elements and keep going; and, in doing so, they provide a background for early spring growth.

White quince is apt to be in bud now, and a sudden drop in temperature can turn the flowers brown. So bring a few branches inside for forcing, and enjoy an early spring. Some early daffodils have had snow hats recently, and crocuses bloomed through it all.

This being a good month for planning and planting trees—always planning first—remember to prune our old friend the crape myrtle if it is out of hand. In fact, this rather bleak month is ideal for shaping it from a fat shrub into a stunning small tree. The same can be done for Burford holly, especially where its lower branches have been ruined by smaller shrubs growing into them. Prune it up, revealing a strong, bare trunk; then shape its top by removing a few thick branches.

Notice what a well-designed brick wall does for the entire lot and how very important the existing clump of hardwoods is to the front lawn. Appreciate what a strong, satisfactory line a wide walk makes from terrace to garden. The two areas might have fallen apart, but instead they draw together.

HEMLOCK

If you delight in huge, blue hydrangea heads, cut back three-fourths of the hydrangea growth now, and scatter your wood ashes, which they love, around the plants.

If you have plans to thin out areas that are too thick and too close to the house, mark sourwoods to be saved, for they are worth saving. Their dried tassels silhouetted against the sky are easy to spot, and their gray, lined, twisted trunks are always among the loveliest things around.

Now that you are thinking of early spring colors, plant doronicums and dwarf bleeding hearts and become acquainted with the very handsome and hardy perennial globe thistle called Echinops.
It is a beauty.

Accomplishing the odds and ends of February gets us under way just in time. Pushy March is blowing around the corner.

*W*INTER *C*HORES

DECEMBER: A superb berry month—
red ones on hollies and dogwoods and
blue clusters on mahonias. Dig now as
long as the soil is workable. Add topsoil
and pinestraw mulch. All bulbs and
well-rooted roses can be planted safely.

JANUARY: An in-between month of planning and planting. Move any shrub needing a new location, and prune deciduous trees that need shaping. All dead limbs can be spotted easily and should be removed, before they come crashing down on shrubs or people. Sow hardy annual seeds of larkspur, cornflowers, and sweet peas *(Lathyrus odoratus)* during breaks in the weather. Christmas rose *(Helleborus niger),* Lenten rose *(Helleborus orientalis),* and early, small daffodils should bloom now.

FEBRUARY: The ultimate test of the winter landscape plan and a month of preparation. Chrysanthemums, pansies, and roses can be planted or moved. Add sand to very heavy soil, and work in fertilizer lightly. Inspect all deciduous shrubs and evergreens for dead wood; shape if necessary. Hydrangeas can be cut back three-fourths of total growth. Reseed bare spots in grass. Cool-weather vegetables such as lettuce, snowpeas, and greens can be planted.

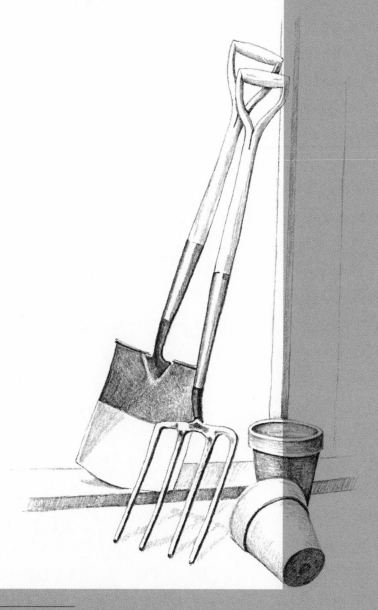

WILD AZALEA

Spring

March · April · May

Before spring intoxicates us with its beauty, take some time in March to double-check your plans. Thoughtful placement of plant material means the difference between success and failure. Azaleas planted on the south side of the house will not be successful unless shaded by trees, but all hollies will accept that exposure. Aucubas are not at their best with western exposures, but they remain a very lush dark green when located on the northeast and northwest sides of houses.

March winds can be rough, but groups of hemlocks act as stunning buffers for daffodils, hyacinths, and pansies. Be sure that the background is limited to one kind of shrub and that early-flowering material is grouped by color. The same splendid results can be achieved year after year with planning. A wild mix of early spring colors looks like a display of plants for sale. The effect is busy and tiring.

Intelligent planting in April softens obvious errors, but it cannot gloss over a basic failure of design. Try to remember that plants must look comfortable where they are asked to grow. For instance, evergreen dwarf *Euonymus radicans* is low and spreading, with shining evergreen foliage that seems to have been waxed. Sunny slopes are exactly its choice, but rule out lanky, tall material here. Thoughtful planting creates the right effect.

The uproar of spring will soon be upon us. Masses of azaleas, beds of tulips, groups of hyacinths, and drifts of dogwood will explode all around us. This abundance can be a gardener's despair. There is still that *Magnolia stellata* on the "want" list, together with just a few of those deep red-pink hyacinths, and at least a start of the white *Pachysandra!* Beat back the urge.

The time has come to realize that nothing else must go in unless something comes out. Guard that balance, or you will lose the subtle curve of the terrace or the happy flow of color outside the living-room window that can be enjoyed year after year. Try to remember the fabulous blooms yet to come. They must be given the space they will demand at their peak. If the basic design pattern is correct, it will assert itself, and the change of seasons will proceed happily.

DAFFODIL

Write a bold note on your calendar during mid-April: **Plant seeds for summer color now!** It will startle you into doing it. Be sure that your time and effort are concentrated where they will do the most good.

Take the case of the homeowner who wanted all of his flowers, regardless of kind and color, in the front yard where he and everyone else could see them. They were seen all right, even when the frost hit them, creating a picture of utter ruin. There is a better way.

Although it will take time, first be absolutely sure that evergreen backgrounds are established and in good scale.

SNOWDROPS

Second, choose only those colors that, without argument, go well with your house (or whatever structure your project involves). Third, place those carefully selected flowers against evergreen backgrounds. Then, the complete scene will be totally satisfying.

Teucrium and lemon thyme add to the beauty of smooth, softly colored paving stones. Thornless locust trees throw fascinating shadows on a smooth wall. Grand Opera cannas planted in April are superb when grouped against clustered evergreens. Smoke trees *(Rhus cotinus)* are a joy as accents in well-designed gardens, and gray-and-green *Santolinas* fill the need of a soft touch by wide steps in constant sunshine.

In May, keep a short rein on flowering shrubs, being careful of their placement. They are not attractive standing alone during fall and winter, but if placed with evergreens and grouped together according to kind, they will easily show to advantage for several months. The hallmark of poor planning is careless use of color in any season. If hot red is one of your favorites, cool it off with plenty of green foliage. Do remember that reds, deep purples, and dark blues are not seen at night, nor are they noticed in late afternoon.

Add to your list of exceptional flowering plants: Reiger begonias in yellow, apricot, and orange; the viburnum Chinese Snowball; and soft pink, white, and Nikko blue garden hydrangeas. Stunning extras that give a lift to shrubs and flowers are supplied by standard redtip photinias, double pink altheas, and gardenias. Then add boxleaf holly, Foster holly, and dwarf Japanese ligustrum to groupings of red and green Japanese and laceleaf maples. For pure visual delight, plant Sunburst locusts and purple-leaf plum trees near a doorway or walk. Just use what you choose sparingly.

Late May has its surprises. If the Arum lily is a stranger, do become acquainted, because its life cycle is fascinating. From late spring it will continue to display red berries, slowly turning to orange,

FLOWERING PURPLE PLUM

and stunning leaves all the way into middle summer. The leaves then die out and come alive again in September, staying green through the winter months. They become the answer to a flower arranger's prayer, for they stay fresh in water for several weeks. Once your patch of Arum lilies has gone through its cycle, it will always be there, year after year.

There are many drought-resistant plants that can pull an otherwise well-balanced design plan through some difficult times. It is a good idea to learn all you can about plants known as "light drinkers," for they will keep a very important area presentable through an extended drought. For instance, artemesia, *Verbena sidalcia,* and salvia simply ignore the water problem and take a few more of their friends along with them.

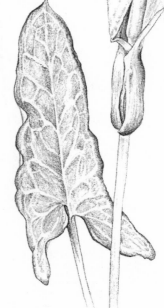

To this group you can add lupine, penstemon, phacelias, and many old varieties of roses. Hibiscus, various herbs, iris, wisteria, and most flowering vines will take care of themselves for a very long time with scant watering. So, where space is available, combine weaker plants with those well known for their history of hardiness. Plants have an uncanny way of helping each other, but all varieties will be given a lift during dry seasons by drip irrigation.

There is no greater satisfaction in landscape design than knowing that certain details are right, that the placement is fine, and that the complete effect is altogether beautiful. A feature that is wrong in some way is a constant bother until the problem is solved. An urn may be too white, a figure too small, a bench too heavy, or a gate too light. But when you finally get the right touch, it shows!

ARUM LILIES

Be careful in the location of details. If they seem to have been there all the time, they are perfect; if they seem strange there or if they look odd, move them. There may not be a suitable setting in your entire present garden for grandmother's sundial. However, if it is really worth using, design an area just for it. Remind yourself that the sundial is to be dominant and plants take second place.

Focal points or other points of interest may be used with success in the direct center of squares, rectangles, or ovals. They can be effective at the end of long walkways against completely closed backgrounds, at crossings as points of lesser emphasis, and in the corners of walls or hedges. Some objects work well flat on the ground enclosed with planting—consider a large, fluted shell surrounded with hosta. There is no problem in introducing a well-chosen focal point, and the more unusual the design, the more interesting the result.

Gracefully hanging, vinelike material easily becomes a fragile and lovely point of interest. Often nothing is needed other than exquisite clematis Ramona or a spray of Harison's yellow rose. Try the miniature variegated euonymus, pink coral vine, or, simplest of all, a thick background of Heavenly Blue morning glories.

Low broadleaf evergreen shrubs are often a perfect complement for elegant details, for they never intrude upon the scene. Beautiful and long-lived choices are mounds of *Ilex cornuta rotunda, Santolina,* and *Ilex helleri.* Perfect details perfectly placed are the secret of a well-balanced design plan.

SHELL AMONG HOSTA

Concentrate on massing the same kind of trees, shrubs, and flowers, using only a few varieties to make the most of their particular beauty. Instead of grouping a dogwood, a red maple, and a crabapple, plant four dogwoods together. Use all white azaleas in that entire bed with groups of pale-pink begonias in front. Always be sure that the azaleas have an evergreen background of one variety of shrub, not eight kinds.

Be aware that this place of yours, planted with a few carefully chosen materials, can acquire a settled beauty in a year's time. Remember that clutter destroys any design plan very quickly. This need never happen if you will heed the warning that where much is going to be planted, much must be taken out. Forewarned is forearmed.

When spring planting is finished, invite the seasons in and enjoy.

CRABAPPLE

MARCH

Color—The Guardian Angel

There are no shortcuts in achieving a successful design for house and garden. Since haste only produces wasted time, take deliberate care in creating a plan with lasting benefits. Seek some professional assistance when you feel the need. It is worth the investment, especially when establishing the basics.

The first two essential ingredients for the successful house and garden are privacy and color. If the lack of privacy is so acute that you cannot be comfortable day by day, there is no way that your design plan will work, no matter how attractive. There must be a well-established enclosure: walls that are beautiful in the dead of winter or shrubs that produce such warmth in their mass of evergreen foliage that their effect alone is a joy.

Color becomes of paramount importance once privacy is achieved. The long-term success of the complete lot now depends on the creative, restrained use of the color combination of trees, flowers, shrubs, and vines. You will experience a triumph if the color harmony is repeated over again in everything that grows throughout your entire plan.

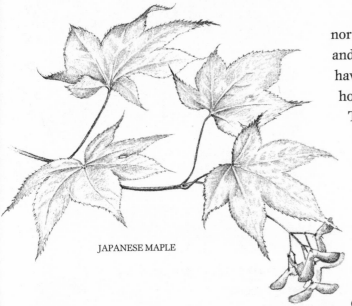

JAPANESE MAPLE

No color pattern simply appears overnight, nor can it develop independently of the house and lot you have as starting points. Suppose you have a light-brown honeywood background of a house and stained chocolate-brown fencing. The natural color harmony to follow would be a combination of bronze, creamy white, yellow, apricot, orange, and red. There would be yellow, white, and orange wild azaleas seen through a gate in semishade, with yellow and white daffodils and crocuses. Tulips in these tones are readily available, as are irises and hybrid daylilies. Japanese broadleaf and cutleaf maples could be featured on their own small pad of bronze *Ajuga* or crab orchard stone. Joseph's coat, tangerine sultana, redhot poker *(Tritoma),* Basket of Gold alyssum, *Rudbeckia, Nicotiana,* chrysanthemums, and small dahlias are luscious additions. A shrub background of cleyera is a natural for this color harmony where walls or fences are not the answer.

There is a key color to every house and garden design, which, when privacy is also attained, blends all parts into a rich, complete composition.

A cutting garden of flowers can be a happy choice as a different approach to color. Here everything grows in rows and bunches with plenty of room for some tomatoes and onions. So why are many unsuccessful? Perhaps because the gardener's ardor collapses in the July sun (plan only the size garden you can enjoy tending), but just as likely because plant varieties were chosen haphazardly. Have you heard someone say that she never really liked red zinnias, but anything that grows so well is a friend of hers? This sort of compromise is not necessary.

Marvelous introductions are appearing in the plant world at such a rate that there is now every conceivable color and size of material anyone could want. If pink is a favorite—and appropriate—color, there is everything from pink-and-white annual salvia and dwarf pink celosia to tiny pink pom-pom dahlias. Varieties are better and choices are greater. The only necessities are fine growing spots, some time with a bit of semishade during the day, and a friable, properly prepared soil.

Many designed plots including flower beds, terraces, walks, and foundation plantings seem to say, "Look, but don't touch." They are lovely and immaculate— brushed, clipped, and sprayed—but somehow they seem to resemble plywood stage settings. Most spaces around any type of house are meant to be used, and they should look as if a human being has passed that way recently. A relaxed outdoor atmosphere helps one live a good life, while stiff spaces with rigid patterns drive one indoors to relax.

Lovely vines close by always take the stiffness out of a planted area. Vines are extroverts and grow with great abandon, as if they enjoy living. Draping over anything handy and spilling their stunning color everywhere, vines work a melting sort of magic. Beautiful designs in paving are warm and congenial and will not be harmed by a bit of traffic as family, friends, and neighbors see a regal lily eye-to-eye or rub elbows with a clump of foxgloves.

Should a low retaining wall be workable, you might create a charming effect with it. Raise the wall above the ground to a sitting height of not more than eighteen inches and top it with a continuous redwood bench and a wide brick or smooth flagstone cap. If there is a source of water nearby, have a small copper tube connected to drop water slowly into a shallow container. While sitting on the bench, watch the show put on by birds of all kinds.

REGAL LILY

Consider a compact area with brick paths, four-foot-wide beds, and perhaps a fountain, sundial, or figure in the middle with a backdrop of peeled cedar or cypress poles and cross-pieces for clematis, morning glories, and climbing roses. After you have completed this design, take a critical look at other sections of the lot with the thought that the usual can be changed into the unusual—not the bizarre—with a little extra time and effort.

A bare terrace may need a redwood trellis built out over part of it with grape vines or wisteria, or both, to break future glare and throw shadows over the surface. Bare walls would welcome hanging baskets, tables and chairs, and a nicely designed flagstone floor ready for steady use.

Think about building steps in an appropriate place, with careful thought as to how to make them beautiful in form and function. Remember this rule for easy, comfortable steps: "Twice the riser plus the tread should equal twenty-six inches."

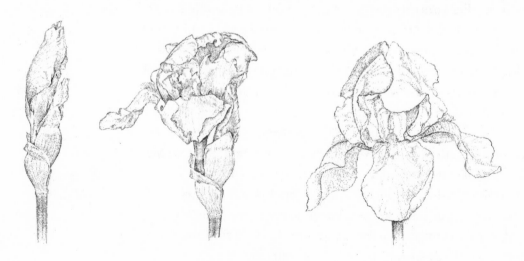

WHITE IRIS

Small Gardens Are Special

Draw a small garden close about you, and watch the unfolding of details with great delight. Such a space often seems to be a room full of its own free spirit, with different moods for each season. One month develops color in a four-by-four bed, moving from white pansies to apricot tulips, then shifting to yellow and orange Reiger begonias. There is no great mystery in creating such a choice spot, only a little homework first on measuring, drainage, sun and shade, paving and edging material, fine detail in trees and shrubs, annuals, and above all, privacy.

A dividend from dealing with a small area is the feeling of belonging within it, for you are in scale with it. Whether, for you, a small space means a secluded, bricked corner with one table, two chairs, and a thick hemlock background or a twenty-foot-square lawn surrounded by cherry trees, interpret it thoughtfully, and its maintenance will be a breeze.

Nothing sets the mood within a small area easier than a choice focal point. So whether you prefer a tranquil stone statue or piece of avant-garde art that might look like a bent pipe to someone else, put it there. This is *your* room.

Maybe no grass at all? Good. How about large squares of different, choice ground covers separated by two-foot-wide walking strips? Even plant annuals in alternate squares, with pine bark for winter. Permanent squares might be planted in green-and-white ivy and variegated *Pachysandra,* while annual squares could display pansies followed by California poppies in sun or dwarf sultanas in shade. If all green is preferred, plant *Hypericum calycinum* in annual squares and fill permanent squares with dwarf evergreen pink-blooming barberry.

PACHYSANDRA

Of course, even a limited area can be done in the traditional grass, flowers, and shrubs—with room for the family—all within forty feet. Every inch counts, so in the beginning, rule out the use of materials that will throw the whole idea out of scale. The smaller the area, the more important to choose materials that have fine texture and individual beauty.

For instance, crab orchard stone is especially beautiful, so, in a confined area, you would certainly want to choose such a material over plain white concrete squares. Use less of a higher quality material rather than more of cheap material whenever possible.

There are ways to create an impression of more space than there really is: use three small plants in a corner instead of one bulging, yellow-green arborvitae; one piece of statuary; one well-shaped evergreen tree with a mat of solid flower color. Provide a smooth texture on the ground of brown pea gravel or pink brick. Consider several vines of one kind trained on a blank wall in a simple square pattern. Perhaps have one hanging basket of trailing rosemary in the sun and one of green-and-white ivy in the shade. All of these solutions will create harmony in color and texture and be a joy to maintain.

Tranquility should be the keynote. Avoid color clashes and grotesque garden sculpture.

The finishing touch is the frame to the picture or walls to the room. Even if all else has gone well, ill-chosen surroundings can kill this small gem of an area. So proceed with care. Whether the choice is an eighteen-inch-high sheared hedge of podocarpus or a three-foot-high wall, let it belong.

CAROLINA YELLOW JESSAMINE

Right Plant, Right Place

Plants have strong characteristics. Like human beings, they react well when they are comfortable, which may require deep shade or no shade, acid soil or sandy soil, a hilltop or shelter from the wind.

You can create a fine design plan that will be successful if you study and understand the wants and dislikes of plants. The textures of plants can be fascinating in certain surroundings and conditions of light. For example, *Mahonia bealei,* Cunninghamia, cryptomeria, aucuba, Chinese holly, *Ilex latifolia,* and yucca look superb in the sun with rough stone or exposed aggregate backgrounds. Wrought-iron backgrounds create a pleasing composition with *Pachysandra* on the ground and Carolina yellow jessamine on the vertical lines.

The fact is that you save dramatically on time, money, and maintenance in the long run when you study the surroundings and the requirements of a given situation. When there is hot sun, the small, brilliant annual portulaca need not be confined to rock gardens or the edges of flower beds. It can also be used on hot, unattractive red clay banks and between and around small junipers as they are developing. The effect is a small sensation! The bank is lovely for a change, and the little plants are building topsoil as they grow.

In every situation, turn what you can to natural advantage. It is a calamity, for instance, to change the natural characteristics of plants by thoughtless pruning. If an osmanthus has been chosen for its handsome, interesting foliage and its preference for semishade, then let it develop as it is meant to, pruning only lightly if a branch decides to be too independent.

Yucca lives on the sun, so watch the choice of pruning shears here. Lapping-type cutters (also called anvil shears) should be banned from use throughout the entire plan except when you are pruning trees, cutting out dead wood, or, for some particular reason, clipping a hedge flat on top and sides.

Consider both sun and shade. Understand the needs of each plant and use both to advantage. Also, remember the variableness of the weather. It is too early to plant seeds outside now because March changes its mind too quickly; but summer annuals can be started in a cold frame or even in the house using small plastic cups and potting soil.

In the Southeast, hollyhocks and sweet William act like perennials by reseeding themselves. Be aware that a balled and burlapped plant is safe if planted now, and this is the time to look for the lovely, pale pink blossoms of the purple-leaf plum.

A Salute to Ivy and Other Vines

Ivy has more devoted friends and sworn enemies than any other known vine. Its adaptability is unsurpassed, which is why it gets into trouble so often. But friends outnumber foes, for ivy actually solves problems in a very attractive way. Surely a good

CAROLINA YELLOW JESSAMINE

thing can be overdone, and so many times this particular vine is found where it has no business being.

If you handle ivy thoughtfully, give it a definite design to follow, and guide it in the right direction, it does a superb job. When ivy is shaped into balls, swags, cones, topiaries, frames, islands, and fences, there seems to be nothing it cannot accomplish —except to stand upright without holding on. It is the gardener's fault if ivy overcomes a house or tree. Any exuberant plant will run wild if ignored.

A standard front lawn can be made smaller and almost work-free if you cover the center with shredded pine bark and surround it with an undulating ivy frame. Give ivy, used in any special composition, at least twelve months to reach maturity and note how it solves innumerable problems with dispatch.

Carolina yellow jessamine, with its bushy top and skinny legs, simply needs someone to watch out and care for it. Part of its tremendous new growth produced by intense heat should be wound back down its main runners and then allowed to flip up and climb again. This little trick will give the plant thickness from the ground up.

If there is a small, bare pine tree nearby, Carolina yellow jessamine will promptly festoon its beautiful yellow flower throughout the branches and down the trunk creating a billowy mass that is quite lovely. Crawling and winding, our fragrant friend goes the entire length of a carport, hanging gracefully across wide openings and unsightly downspouts, but it overwhelms mailboxes.

Clematis, the aristocrat, creates such beauty in all of its forms that it is well worth struggling with. Do give it shade on its feet and sun on its head and a small area to climb.

In springtime, use the following annual vines in sun or semishade: mixed Japanese morning glories, scarlet runner beans, *Thunbergia* (black-eyed Susan vine), moonflowers, mixed cypress vine, and marble vine. Give them a large trellis and let them mingle with each other. You will have an effortless, fun time, and you will be reminded that the oft-forgotten vines can soften the world.

APRIL

The Older House

When buying an old house, keep in mind that it has belonged to others for years. It may be difficult for a while to establish your own identity, but persevere. Clear areas, change plant material, and overcome amazing color mixtures that are hard to live with. Press forward until your family's personality emerges.

Very often you can be grateful that former owners left fine plants—even though there may be so many of them that you need an expeditionary force to discover the basic plan. When plants are obviously of inferior quality, it is actually easier to remove them and redesign the cleared lot.

Today there is a better understanding of how to handle very shady and very hot areas. Nothing needs to wither away slowly in a forgotten dark hole by a side door, nor does any plant—unless it was collected from a desert—need to be left in hot, boiling sun. There is plant material available now for every conceivable situation; just choose carefully.

Deep shade happily covering paved sitting areas welcomes groups of potted plants that can be moved about. If relentless sun is the problem, especially over new flower beds, fast-growing shade trees will easily provide light shadows.

Be certain that you are following a plan, an existing one that you "inherited" or a new one that you have devised yourself. You can rejoice if the design plan in place is so comfortable that you can slip right into it. But if you have to guess what comes next, create your own design plan and stick with it.

Remember: Every design plan must be based on reason, have a theme, and reduce maintenance to a minimum. Plans should be clear-cut guides to a simpler and more enjoyable way of living. Keep this ideal in mind.

Whatever you do, remember to stay in character with the house. For instance, it is a shock to landscape architects and historians to see a series of abstract metal figures featured throughout the garden area of an Early American house. And, it would be a travesty to ruin the setting of a Spanish-style house by including an Early American dooryard garden.

A concrete walk through fine woodlands is a thoughtless mistake, but pine bark paths with wood edges are a delight. So, be alert to what is incongruous and inappropriate. Be reminded that you can create stunning effects by surrounding distinctive architecture with outdoor design plans that are in character. It is sad, indeed, to behold a distinguished Georgian house intentionally (but uncomfortably) surrounded by rugged rock gardens and rambling zinnia beds.

When in doubt, research the architectural style of your house and follow that lead. If it is difficult to identify the period and style, ask for help in studying the house's strongest characteristics, and then emphasize them with good taste. This sort of research can be very rewarding, and a landscape architect can be very helpful here.

Houses and lots that have nothing in their favor but good drainage can still be made colorful, interesting in detail, and very livable. Absolute authenticity in design is not necessary, but all parts of the whole certainly must blend.

Until the color of the house blends well with its roof, doors, and shutters, there is no point in working on its evergreen frame or foreground. An "off" color will pull the other details apart. Once color is settled, your progress in following a coherent plan can

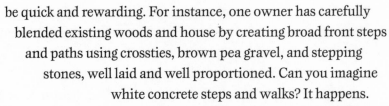

be quick and rewarding. For instance, one owner has carefully blended existing woods and house by creating broad front steps and paths using crossties, brown pea gravel, and stepping stones, well laid and well proportioned. Can you imagine white concrete steps and walks? It happens.

Let me elaborate on that dependable rule for steps: Twice the riser plus the tread should equal twenty-six inches. For example, a six-inch riser times two equals twelve inches; that means a tread of fourteen inches will give you the desired total of twenty-six. Four-inch risers call for eighteen-inch treads. Use this rule to compute the dimensions that fit your space, and you will never have impossible, awkward steps.

When considering color blending, a house of the traditional red brick calls for special care. Just suppose you have one surrounded by original groups of redbud (Judas) trees. Now, visualize how much more effective those distinctive purplish blooms would be if they were gradually shifted out among existing pines and hardwoods some distance from the house. If you have no redbuds and want some, plant them, one at a time, scattering them through pines, maples, and other flowering trees. Just be sure that they are not located anywhere near a *red* brick house.

Another note of caution: Be wary of planting your favorite flowering shrubs (such as forsythia or hydrangea) in front of the house or in any open area. Such favorites are bare in winter. Give them a background of handsome walls or fences to frame the design plan and soften the bleak look of bare twigs and shriveled foliage and flower heads.

Take time in April to notice all shrubs. Count the flowering ones—such as the forsythia, quince, spirea—which too often become sandwiched among the evergreens. Plan to pluck out these shrubs and relocate them, grouped according to variety, in sunny spots along a fence, against the garage, or as a background for the entire area. With these shifts you will enjoy rich, concentrated color instead of lonesome polka-dots.

Next, notice the evergreens themselves. Plan to shift tall *Camellia sasanqua, Photinia glabra,* and all Burford hollies toward the end of the house wall. Then go hunting for dwarf broadleaf *Ilex helleri* or *Ilex compacta* to cluster on each side of the front door area. Consider a group of six or eight pittosporums under a low front window. Ignore spreading junipers, all too available and persistent, for they can produce monotony in a hurry. Turn, instead, to dwarf yaupon holly, *Ilex helleri,* and *Santolina*—three superb evergreens that belong at the front of the house.

It is very comforting to think of having a beautiful, workable plan close by. This means that impractical and distracting ideas have already been tossed outside into a very stiff wind. Now, with just a little quiet thought and attention to detail, you will achieve more beauty with your own shrubs, trees, flowers, and vines than you ever dreamed possible.

Always look with a critical eye to ensure harmony throughout, and discover the splendid possibilities waiting to be chosen. Relax all over and enjoy.

Handling the Trouble Spots

All houses and lots have troublesome areas. These problems can be solved if you study each one carefully, not only on its own terms but also as an interrelated part of the whole.

There may be steep sunny banks or totally shady corners by house walls; you may be defied by a narrow strip of soil in the middle of a driveway or steps so steep

HOSTA BLOOM

that nobody uses them. There is no end to possible nightmares, but it is never too late to produce a plan of attack and defeat these obstacles to beauty and comfort.

In that narrow driveway strip, plant evergreen dwarf ivy, completely hardy and easy to maintain. Another option is to pave the strip with an attractive pattern of brick or stone. Attack steep, sunny banks with spreading pyracantha (Santa Cruz variety), or go with dwarf ivy here, also. There is an extra dividend that comes with the pyracantha: it forms fine color patterns both in spring with flowers and in fall with its berries, which are loved by mockingbirds and robins.

Turn any totally shady corners by the house into assets by planting some of the many exotics that must never be planted in sunny spots. Choose hostas of different varieties, lily of the valley, large and small mahonia, aucuba, bleeding hearts, Virginia bluebells, caladiums, coleus, and *Sarcococca*—to name a few.

A thick blanket of shade is actually one of the easier problems to solve. Start noticing shady spaces wherever you go, not only the forlorn ones, but also the lovely ones, rich in texture and color. Make notes of the vines, trees, ground covers, and flowers that make such spaces beautiful.

In shady or sunny spots, planter boxes and pots can solve problems by providing additional options. For example, leave enough room between plants in shade to slip in pots of tuberous pink or white dwarf begonias, caladiums, crotons (colored ornamental foliage), or coleus. In sun, use petunias or geraniums in the same way.

You do need to be careful to water plants in containers, which dry out quickly. A simple solution with planter boxes is to attach a section of perforated hose along the back of the box and turn on as needed.

Very often a well-espaliered plant, meticulously and carefully pruned against a wall or fence, will hold an entire planter box together. You need add only dwarf evergreens and ivy at the base of the featured plant. Excellent material for espaliers

AZALEA AND GERANIUM IN AN OLD TIN TUB

include pyracantha, loropetalum, cleyera, mahonia, anise, *Euonymus kewensis,* and small English ivy.

Woodlands are simply vast groups of trees, but they can be enchanted forests. Practically speaking, they are totally enjoyable only if there is no overgrowth of grass or weeds or thickets of unwanted seedlings. There must be areas that one can wander through at will, enjoying nature and escaping into timelessness. If this description does not match your woodland, start planning.

Establish a visible, generous path four feet wide, beginning near the house and leading to a natural opening, perhaps by a stream. If there is no such stream, consider making an artificial water feature. Plant or sow seeds of wildflowers on both sides of the path. Make the shady clearing at the end of the path large enough to accommodate two or more chairs, one dog, and one cat. What a joy!

So much is growing in even the smallest woodland that it might be more comfortable to take one step at a time in developing your little forest. Where there is a thicket of pines, thin them out so a few hardwoods such as oak, hickory, and maple can be added. Leave space for several blooming trees, perhaps redbud, dogwood, crabapple, fringe tree (graybeard), and silver bell *(Halesia)*. It may be that three of the largest pines would be enough to leave, depending entirely on existing space, size, and the amount of constant shade needed.

Go one step further and plant several native shrubs, beginning with buckeye, oakleaf hydrangea, wild azaleas, and box myrtle. Then plan to add native vines and flowers near the sitting area if possible. Of course, if you are fortunate enough to have a treasure trove of these materials already established, you need only remove unwanted competitors.

DOGWOOD

Now, delight in your enchanted forest, and walk through it in all seasons.

If you have inherited a scarred, clear-cut area where the old forest floor is eroding, your priority is to find the quickest and best way to hold the soil. If you do not come to the rescue, the topsoil will wash away, and the ground will crack open during the next drought. Although you deal first with the emergency, don't forget to plan and mark places for new shade trees.

The simplest way to stop erosion is to plant grass. No one, however, wants to cut grass on steep slopes or rugged ground; so use your knowledge of ground covers. Plant low-maintenance evergreen dwarf mondo or dwarf ivy where grass is inappropriate. Don't ignore gravity by counting on pine bark chunks, chips, or pellets, which will simply wash away and pile up on lower levels.

Hot sun around houses is made more bearable with a green ground cover of whatever kind you choose. If there is more space for grass than you need or want to mow, divide the area. Have a small lawn near the house. In larger, more remote spaces, sow grasses that will grow bushy and tall, resembling a meadow. Broadcast seeds of cornflowers, poppies, coreopsis, and crotalaria throughout, and they will bloom through the tall grass.

Existing open woodland floors that will gradually revert to woods have a way of sprouting hundreds of volunteers. Treat these with respect, for a while at least. Native honeysuckle is valuable when there is nothing else to hold the soil, as are native huckleberries. Plants that are likely to reappear include ivy planted sixty years ago and the ever-present eleagnus, which is loved mostly by birds.

Get busy with selective cutting where the growth is crowded and mixed. Leave only the choicest trees, like sourwoods and crabapples, and plan your view. Hold the soil with a mulch of leaves, pine straw, and hay. The woods will return, and the results will be worth the work.

MAY

A House in the City

Some city lots are instantly charming, while others offer a catalogue of flaws. Note a meandering grass strip on the edge of the trees. It seemingly has no beginning and no particular end, and obviously has never had any care. Another detraction might be ivy spreading in every direction with nothing to contain it. You may find that a well-intentioned person has cut squares in the grass for flower beds without taking steps to keep the grass out of the flowers. Sometimes one can see trees that are slowly dying because power mowers frequently nick the unprotected trunks.

Each of these defects can easily be remedied. Brick edging can contain the grass and the ivy, and ground cover can encircle and protect the trees. If you are bedeviled with rampant honeysuckle in trees, poison ivy in the English ivy, thin grass with no topsoil, and gullies in every direction, simply solve these problems, one by one, with sound planning.

You can make a great difference in just one season if you attack weeds and rejuvenate the grass with topsoil, fertilize, plant seeds, and water. If needed, put in a drainage and water system as soon as possible. Then come the added touches: well-laid brick edges, retaining walls, ground covers—the details of your long-term design plan.

Be grateful, of course, if this sort of design plan is already in place—the result of time and dedication. Each element meshes into the next, so that no space floats alone, and no planting wanders off into infinity with nothing to stop it.

City lots developed to their highest potential can have a different mood for each passing season. Each design is different, of course, and people's tastes can be poles apart. The one element that tells all, in every situation, is scale. A trained eye can tell in a second if an urn or bench is too small or too large, but if you have never had the opportunity to use accessories before, how do you begin?

First, remember that scale outdoors is different from scale indoors—there are no walls and ceilings, just space. Next, develop the habit of standing far off to study a bench, steps, or a wall. This is the most helpful secret of all: do not study an object or area "eyeball to eyeball." Move away and allow light, shadow, and air to show you what an area can accommodate.

You must take the time to study and restudy. Confidence is gained slowly by experimenting and changing and looking. Going through this process develops your "eye." It becomes obvious that the bench over there is exceedingly small, and the cluster of stone or concrete mushrooms are uncomfortable where they are. Now, if those mushrooms are given a small woodland corner all to themselves with a light cover of foliage in the back holding them steady, the composition is entirely different and delightful!

But, mushrooms floating on the lawn? Never. And painted? Perish the thought.

Think of this outdoor living space as an uncluttered, indoor living room. Begin furnishing it with one or two good pieces—perhaps beautiful outdoor chairs or a bench. Subordinate all else to them. Pick colors and shapes and sizes with the same care as you add other items, not only wood, metal, and stone objects, but also shrubs and trees. Plant carefully and thoughtfully as you create a livable design, a great part of which may be quite permanent.

We can move on from the old-fashioned arbor, which in bygone days was made of light pieces of wood and repaired and painted each year. Now an arbor can be constructed of metal with welded joints, painted black to "disappear" and planted with several glorious climbing roses. Enjoy it forever!

White wooden benches in the shade of trees—so dear to the hearts of our grand-parents—are now often beautifully fashioned of aluminum or weathered wood or woven strips of nylon or plastic. They can remain outdoors for twelve months and need only a quick going over with a cloth or sponge to keep them in good shape.

Enhance the charm of this outdoor living space with choice plants. By all means choose several dwarf evergreen plants to group on each side of a bench; their placement will never seem to be an afterthought.

A word of caution: Shun the bizarre. Remember concrete stepping stones in the shape of giant footprints, jolly little dwarfs, lions spitting water, frogs whose eyes light up, and the tall, skinny pink flamingos. Though it seems the grotesque will always be with us, heaven forbid taking it seriously in your landscape design.

Gazebos have great charm; swings are delightful; wood seesaws for children are more aesthetically pleasing than circus-colored play sets; bridges are useful and decorative. But, remember, they all cannot be used on a single fifty-foot lot. Go easy.

Water is always an attraction. Pumps and pools are better than ever now, and blooming water plants are available in all shades of vivid colors. Find out the latest from books, garden-club programs, nurseries, or landscape architects.

If we have learned one thing from the past, it is that chaos is apt to reign when too many delightful possessions are placed in the yard. Select the very best, such as a weatherproof picnic table with benches. Sturdy and well-designed, this little grouping will create no problems and will provide enduring charm.

The placement of plant material takes a combination of self-control and design sense —attributes we all cultivate continually. Weeping willows are in the shadows of many a memory; so are moss roses, peonies, and mother's lilacs. All are available in stronger varieties today, but do not let nostalgia overwhelm you. Don't use them all at once.

After parts of a design plan are changed, there always seem to be various scattered shrubs and trees left over. You may find yourself with several odd-sized abelias,

weigelas, arborvitaes, a dozen January jessamines, and three frozen pyracanthas. Perhaps they have been used in the wrong way or placed in a difficult exposure or forgotten. Double-check the possibilities for each one.

Abelias are excellent when used as low-cut, well-fed hedges, but they are a total loss as specimen shrubs because they have no interesting detail. Weigelas take a tremendous amount of space, so do not try to use them on a small lot. For large spaces, they are delightful in collections of eight to ten as backgrounds for smaller shrubs or to mark property boundaries.

Arborvitaes need plenty of sun and should always be grouped informally, not set in straight lines. January jessamine *(Jasminum nudiflorum)* can become so entangled with long Bermuda grass and weeds that it will drive even a mild-tempered person wild. Unless it can be set in a well-edged bed, jessamine will not be completely satisfactory, but it is fine for hanging over and softening bare walls, impossible steps, and sunny banks. And the damaged pyracanthas? Discard them.

Almost all odd plants can be useful somewhere on your property, so look around before passing them along to a friend or tossing them away. Keep in mind that three or four of any variety are almost always easier to use than one lone plant.

A House in the Country

Home owners with a country setting think on a larger scale than those in the city. Trees on distant hills are often their focal points, rather than a bench ten feet away. Ponds of water and rolling hills require that a design plan be casual and loose, with enough space to coast beautifully over to living areas without throwing any part of the plan out of scale.

If you are building in the country for the first time, it will help to keep your mind clear of any set type of planting design. Let the house, the land, and existing growth from trees to native shrubs suggest the key to the successful blending of the old with the new. Make no mistake—a blending must occur or the countryside will seem to reject this new neighbor.

Study native plants, remembering that they are the hardiest of all and obviously like the soil. Develop a pine grove of different varieties surrounded by native broadleaf evergreens. There is constant delight in its beauty and ease of maintenance.

Relish the rich heritage of native plants. American hollies are native, as are sumac, sourwood, magnolia, leucothoe, Scotch broom, fern, and wild azalea. You will create the most successful design if you group plants of the same kind in masses. The acreage around this country house is not going to give out. Where you would set spirea six feet apart in the city, use eight to ten feet in the country.

When looking from a distance, it is visually pleasing to see space in between groupings. But remember to connect one group to another and to the house by adding extra plants where necessary, so the house will never seem to float in a lonely sea. Remember, also, to reduce the scale of plants near the house, where the house is the focal point, not the plants.

Consider a plan that would place the house on a rich pad of ivy, grass, or dwarf mondo. Plant groups of Burford holly at front and back corners only, then let trees and shadows do the rest. The same green pad at the base of house walls will control any splash; then the house is free to settle itself, blending easily with surrounding areas.

New construction is the time when an owner's choice of designer and design is absolutely vital, and the designer certainly may be yourself. Or you may choose to work, at least in part, with a professional.

Go slowly, be sure, and be concerned. Think of colorful native materials—of stone, oak, and pine, and plan to repeat these natural colors inside. The entire countryside will then accept house and setting as "belonging." This sense of belonging is the test of a perfect blend.

Garden Perfume

Anyone who has walked near a crabapple tree lately knows that spring has come. The haunting perfume of lilacs is with us, and we are just enjoying our last tulips. A few weeks ago there was the unforgettable perfume from *Viburnum carlcephalum* and *Magnolia stellata,* as well as hyacinths and daffodils. Now all around us is the heavy fragrance of Carolina yellow jessamine.

The fragrance of flowers has always delighted one of our richest senses, the sense of smell. Various botanical gardens have fragrant sections designed especially for the visually impaired, and garden perfume can be the focus of your own design plan.

When selecting varieties for fragrance in garden or border, remember to handle heavy perfume lightly with a few plants, but use a mass of growth for delicate fragrances. Give these plants space to be seen and smelled. Groups of heliotrope surrounded by green-and-white *Pachysandra* with a foreground patch of grass are not only a feast for the eye, but also an absolute dessert for the nose.

Summer nights are the finest possible settings for tall groups of *Nicotiana* in pots or borders close to a terrace. White moonvines covering trellises and entire walls blend their fragrance on the night air so hauntingly that noses twitch for miles around.

By all means be sure to design your fragrant garden area so that it is as delightful to sniff in the early morning as in the evening. Clay pots of lemon verbena, lavender, applemint, and Sunset ivy (actually a trailing variety of geranium) can be kept in the shade all day and transferred to a terrace or patio in the evening.

MOONFLOWER

The fragrance of perennial phlox, peonies, vitex, and crape myrtle and the clear, tangy smell of lantana are with us all summer. At the end of summer you can taper off with late gladiolus and the elusive fragrance of eleagnus flowers to carry you through the early fall.

The secret of the successful fragrance plot is simple, open space. There should be no clutter, only beauty and wafting perfume to be enjoyed at leisure until the first chilly night moves through as a gentle reminder that it is time to rest.

Outdoor Rooms

An original touch can give outdoor areas your personal "decorator" stamp. The personal touch makes a difference with mailboxes, garbage cans, and light posts. House numbers can attract or repel. You can lift driveways out of the ordinary. There is always room for originality without being outlandish, without resorting to such oddities as miniature volcanoes set among boulders, mailboxes set atop plows, and entrance gates straight out of Hansel and Gretel.

If you are working with a builder, beware of the phrase, "You don't do it that way; it's not on the plan." Anything you want to do that is a little different, much less original, will throw this builder; and the time to communicate is sooner rather than later. Call a halt to everything, sit down with the person in charge, and find out just exactly what is included in the plan and contracts. Search out every detail.

Remember that your house, apartment, condominium, or office building is only a part of the overall outdoor design. Features other than the building itself have important design aspects, too. There must be a clear understanding in the blueprint stage concerning widths and lengths of terraces or patios, the position of air conditioners and utility meters, heights and widths of steps, the material to be used in steps and walkways, and where walls will or will not be built.

Plan, plan, plan *with* your builder. You do not have to accept a three-foot-wide, white concrete walk meandering in from the wrong direction or a generic promise of "bushes" set against the building in stiff rows. You do not have to accept such things unless they are specified on the plan that you approve. If they get past the planning stage, then you must pay to correct such problems. Well-laid plans provide a canvas for originality.

Take time to think through color harmonies of both building materials and plant materials. Be aware of the textures of brick and stone outside as well as wood and tile inside. Even consider the colors of rugs and draperies.

Builders or owners certainly have the right to add a whimsical detail. It might be a specially designed street number in front. Just be very sure that it works and adds to the whole.

There can be a timeless beauty in muted tones of brick and stone or in the natural grace of one fine tree standing alone. Well-placed features mean more through the years than flower beds that are indifferently tended. But do not miss having flowers. They offer the opportunity to be creative in literally hundreds of ways with minimum cost.

You might plan and plant a sedate garden of summer annuals. First mark off a size that can be cared for without agony. Frame the area simply with a clipped abelia hedge or, if it pleases you, do it gloriously with columns and trellises on all four sides. Your quiet garden may be a ten-foot square, a 40-foot-by-20-foot rectangle, an ellipse, or a circle, but make it fit the site and make it yours.

If a flower bed is not the love of your life, an alternative might be masses of color in pots, which could be grouped anywhere. Even within the smallest area, you can have the beauty and inspiration of flowers.

SPRING CHORES

MARCH: A month to hold steady, for March winds can be rough. One of the first jobs to accomplish in garden areas is the planting of bush roses. They feel comfortable outside now, especially when they are pruned neatly and cleared of any crossed branches.

Whenever the wind slows down, divide any perennials that obviously need it, such as phlox and dwarf coreopsis, and relocate some to those bare spots that have always been a bother. Larkspur, calliopsis, and cornflowers are ready to be transplanted now if you planted seeds in the fall. In the middle of March, plant seeds of carrots, snow peas, and Bibb lettuce if you like to have your own cool-weather vegetables, but wait a few days if the soil is wet.

Keep a sharp eye out for any intrusion on the design plan and also for any improvements you want to consider. Remember your stunning friend the hemlock, which not only is beautiful, but also can be a perfect wind buffer where March reveals that you need one. Try one out in your sketchbook, and add it to your plan if it will work. Be true to your strategy and you will make no mistakes as you plant additional shrubs and flowers. They will be a delight to see and a joy to maintain.

APRIL: A month of great dividends if you keep your entire design plan in balance. If plants of all kinds, evergreen and deciduous, seem to be sprouting up all over the place, get out the plan and check everything. Be sure to care for those plants that need protection, but be ruthless in removing unplanned "extra dividends," which in their seasonal exuberance threaten to overcrowd and overcome the intended effect.

Plant seeds now for flowers such as the newly improved zinnia family so that you can look forward to the pleasure of seeing them all summer long. Take a leisurely trip to several nurseries and farmers' markets and select plants from their stock of colorful annuals and perennials that are potted up or in flats and ready to be located in the appropriate places when you return home. This is an enormously convenient service and saves hours of time. Another miracle timesaver and spring gift to yourself is dwarf mondo. Use it anywhere you want an evergreen lawn that requires no mowing—ever.

MAY: The month to plant any annual on your "must" list. Do include rows of dahlias for cutting, and use their colorful blooms to fill flat containers on coffee tables and in the center of the dining room table. Don't forget to plant marigolds and celosia. Spring blooms will become waves of color through July and August until frost. Watch for weeds now, and clear them out while they are small. Also check drainage in all planted beds. We can do without rot and mildew.

GINKGO

Summer

June · July · August

Trees are now in their glory. Their shapes and shadows are beautiful; severe weather has not hurt them, and they are ready to accomplish wonders. Striking lace-leaved ginkgoes will even have a second act later when their rich green foliage changes to pure gold. Dawn cypress, Japanese evergreen oaks, zelkovas, and chestnut oaks are on dress parade. Sugar maples are ready, accompanied by black gum *(Nyssa sylvatica)*, which is loved for its flowers and the rich honey made from them.

Dogwood is a constant friend, in groups or alone, but beware of keeping box elder trees *(Acer negundo)* too long—unless they are the only trees on the place—for they are neither strong nor beautiful and multiply like weeds. Turn your thoughts instead to the graceful, native river birches.

Do not let summer tempt you to go to a nursery or farmers' market and buy a dozen of every bloom in sight. Instead, remember that summer wildflowers are all around us and nothing is more beautiful. A field of coreopsis and daisies is a design unto itself as are roadsides striped in orange with butterfly weed *(Asclepias)* glowing in the hot sun. You could not plan a more delightful sight than native Queen Anne's

Lace (wild carrot) billowing along woodland roads and paths and the often shunned, common orange daylily having a moment of glory everywhere.

Volunteer reseeded larkspurs and cornflowers are perfectly happy by anyone's fence down the road, by the wall, or up the hill. And the magnificent oakleaf hydrangeas are one of the real glories of early summer.

One does not deliberately plan for wildflowers or for wild shrubs and trees but accepts them year after year and enjoys the stunning results. There is no guesswork, for they have lived here longer than you have, and they never disappoint.

Wildflowers will be very glad to bloom and grow where they are really wanted and often where they are not, just to make things interesting! If you transplant or overseed wildflowers, do mulch and water at first. Then after they have begun, they will like very much to be left alone. Please, please buy native plants from a responsible nursery that does not get them from the wild—and never dig them up yourself!

One person's weed is another's treasure. Our native jimson weed (*Datura* or Angel's Trumpet) is known as a fine exotic along the east coast. Groups of the huge trumpets create excitement in a handy corner. There is no plant that holds stream banks better than the common daylily. Butterfly weed is famous for stopping erosion in its tracks, and it is added to perennial borders in the east as a prized possession.

There is one and only one way to handle natives—casually. They absolutely refuse to stay within a formal design, so do not ask it of them. Let them flop and wander and reseed and come up willy-nilly, and everything around will be all the more beautiful because of their presence.

Note the many visual delights as late spring gives way to early summer. The beautiful tree blooming with a great profusion of yellow flowers is the Golden Rain Tree. Originally from China, Korea, and Japan, it grows anywhere and is not particular about soil. There are also great mounds of white oakleaf hydrangeas in full bloom. Preferring semishade, these tough, native shrubs form fine screens in summer and excellent backgrounds for masses of daylilies.

Evergreen Andora junipers cascade over walls with the greatest of ease—a good example of the right plant in exactly the right place. Excellent evergreen vines such as southern smilax bring charm to stiff lines, and standard topiary trees turn plain doorways into fine focal points. No house or grounds can, or should, be a cold copy of another. Notice what flourishes. Let an area tell you what it needs and what it wants to do, and problems will disappear while June leads you happily along into summer.

July is a time when we devoutly wish that garages, parking areas, and cars could drop through trap doors, leaving only calm, green, uncluttered surfaces. Wishes will not come true magically, but a planting plan for these areas can accomplish a lot.

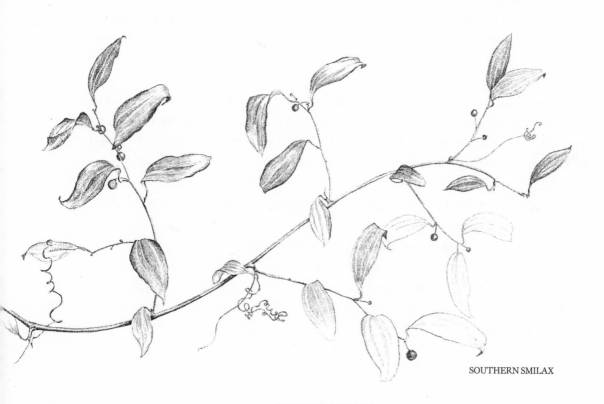

SOUTHERN SMILAX

When carports are shaded by trees with ground-cover carpets, they do not loom up as eyesores. Instead, they settle down and become a lesser part of the scene. Aid the transformation with driveway tracks of brick instead of concrete, filling the center strip with brown pea gravel. Plan to add clipped, evergreen holly trees ten to twelve feet apart on each side, even surrounding any switchback.

Perhaps a garage could possess a handsome roof. If lattice were nailed to its sides, it would be a lovely place for evergreen Carolina yellow jessamine to climb or for attached espaliered holly. Then the garage, regardless of its size, becomes a versatile part of the scene.

As the heat of midsummer persists, be sure that you never have a thick crust on top of the soil in your flower beds. Use a hoe to keep the soil loose, and water using a hose without a nozzle, letting water soak in gently. Consider an irrigation system; if the ease of watering protects your investment in plant materials, the system could pay for itself in the long run.

Broadleaf evergreens can be counted on to thrive through a hot August (unless someone has forgotten to water). How satisfying to imagine the striking, cool, green-and-white hollies growing into thick shrubs of just the height you want. How refreshing now to have *Camellia sasanqua* espaliered on brick walls and dwarf evergreen azaleas in groups to make sharp, ugly corners charming. Enjoy the deciduous pink-flowering cherries that in summer are stunning shade trees and the mimosas that resemble lacy, pale green umbrellas.

Roses are supposed to rest now, but if they insist on blooming, enjoy! Zinnias are still at work in the most fantastic colors. So are crape myrtles, phlox, marigolds, and glads. You can still buy portulaca seeds and plant them where you will be able to see them come up in three weeks. Also, check on such fascinating subjects as annuals and special perennials.

A few "do nots": Do not plant pyracantha in the shade. Do not expect a climbing Peace rose to look very happy on a fragile trellis; it needs a very sturdy arbor. Do not espalier *Camellia sasanqua* or loropetalum on lattice against walls with large, rough stones. Choose the heavier loquat and mahonia. When a wall simply needs to be covered, the small-leaf ivy will be delighted to oblige.

Always have a good reason before you train any plant, including Burford holly and oakleaf hydrangea, into an unnatural shape. An odd, eccentric shape has absolutely no charm and never blends with the whole design. If you discover, however, that a well-known plant such as *Camellia japonica* has a real ability to mimic an evergreen vine on a wall when it is carefully attached and pruned, try it. The result here is a lovely blooming evergreen tracery across vertical areas needing a special touch.

The key to success when handling living, growing material is to understand that plants, too, have personalities and have a great instinct to fulfill their destinies. Learn from them and be humble.

J U N E

A Feast for the Senses

Birds, bees, and all crawlers are drawn to delicious nectar in June. Alerted by perfume, color, and seasonal bloom, gardeners throughout the South and up and down the East Coast learn early on that bees have first choice during blooming periods. This may be a hazardous time for gardeners who have filled entire beds with one variety of intensely fragrant plants. It is difficult not to be unsettled by a solid cover of bees!

In terms of living peacefully with the insects, this beautiful month is far more enjoyable when you include several plant varieties that blend in texture, color, and perfume. Then the busy insects will be distributed among many plants, affording you the opportunity to work among them with some leisure to cut and smell.

Experiment on that carefully executed plan with groups of high, medium, and low flowers, shrubs, and trees. Select those that are at their height of bloom during these beautiful summer months. You will be rewarded with the haunting mystery of perfume floating through annuals, perennials, trees, shrubs, and vines.

All plants are different, and the great puzzle is how and why. In early spring, for example, a delicate fragrance triggers a search that terminates in the discovery that it is produced by one of the smallest blooms of all, the violet. It is fascinating to learn that fragrance has nothing to do with size, color, shape, or weather. Many plants keep their aromatic secrets well into the climax of their lives, which is most often the bloom.

VIOLET

Clutter in the arrangement of plant material chokes growth and smothers fragrance. Individual plants and groups of plants need space that is theirs alone. So, leave breathing space and clear out unwanted material.

An unclipped row of the well-known, hardy, easy-to-grow abelia (which was introduced into the United States in 1844) will guard flower beds and play areas while showing off its pretty, pale pink flowers. It does not beckon you over, but holds its perfume until you brush by—then its fragrant secret is out! The elegant, evergreen Fortune osmanthus, offering white perfumed blooms among deep green foliage, needs a protected location in mountain areas, as does the magnolia.

Fragrance offers a whole new creative dimension in all seasons. There is no monotony in a long walkway flanked on both sides by tall junipers, dwarf magnolias, or boxwoods. The aroma of their crisp, clean foliage is a constant delight. So is the fragrance of yews and, in early spring, a ground cover of snowdrops *(Galanthus)*.

Night fragrance is haunting and heavenly. Do not let one more June go by without planting seeds of pure white moonvines. Then stand by as dusk settles over late afternoon and watch the silent miracle of flowers unfolding and releasing their perfume. It is a benediction for the end of the day.

Peonies beckon in early morning. The snowdrops and the *Gaillardia* (named after M. Gaillard de Mortentgonezau, a patron of botany and South Carolina native of French ancestry) present a clear fragrance during the entire day. Hosta joins them. First introduced in 1790, hosta is the plaintain lily, which now seems to be perfectly happy in the entire United States except the desert.

SNOWDROP

For delicious smells and tastes, nature offers the *Fragaria* or strawberry (so named because of the straw laid between plants to protect the fruit in wet weather) and, of course, the grape, celebrated even in biblical times (". . . and Noah planted a vineyard").

Another delightful addition to your plan might be the fragrant *Halesia,* known as the silver bell tree, with its graceful, drooping habit. It even accepts poor soil, but it does like to be planted near water. Close by there could be the fragrant favorite *Hamamelis mollis,* or witch hazel, which can be grown as a shrub or small tree. Its flowers during early winter are a rich, deep yellow. Under these trees the delightfully fragrant white or blue hyacinth *(Muscari)* can spread its beautiful spring ground cover for many years.

TRUMPET
HONEYSUCKLE

Did you know that honeysuckle *(Lonicera),* which grows all over the country, attracts mockingbirds, robins, brown thrashers, towhees, and bluebirds? That hummingbirds love abelia, azaleas, *Kolwitzia* (beauty bush), *Buddleia,* trumpet vine, and weigela? That *Clethra* (sweet pepper bush) has remarkable, sweet-scented flowers in July and August, and that several of summer's most fragrant roses are Crimson Glory, Etoile de Hollande, Radiance, Mirandy, and Golden Dawn?

The following fragrant annuals and perennials are among the hardiest in the United States: sweet peas, larkspurs, pinks, sweet alyssum, candytuft, nasturtiums, pansies, irises, peonies, *Phlox divaricata,* and heliotrope. There are some great combinations, too. Keep in mind Queen Anne's Lace (native to the southeast) with white azaleas, white peonies, and white foxglove.

SWEET PEA

What riches surround us! Treat them gently and they will provide a constant feast for the senses.

Personality Profile

A garden that has a personality all its own begins as a carefully developed plan, but your design certainly will evolve over a period of time. You will change it, correct it, add to it as you learn and observe more about design, horticulture, and your own property. Take your time, and experiment with the elements of the plan until you have brought all parts of the property into harmony.

There are some rules of design that can guide you from the beginning. For instance, a stationary background can be tremendously helpful. A low wall of brick or stone can be counted on to anchor a developing design regardless of time or weather. Or, use medium-height, broadleaf evergreens for the same purpose—chosen to blend with the plan, hold it together, and create interest in texture and color.

Working ahead on this personality profile of your garden certainly beats actual digging and moving on the ground—likely to occur when plants are ready but plans are not. And consider walks as carefully as plants. A brick or flagstone pattern should be studied and considered thoroughly before you make a decision, because walks are one of the most important details of the entire garden area. They should have at least an easy four-foot width and be located with great care.

Indicate on your layout special locations for benches and for groups of flowering shrubs that will be in the background. Put a pink dogwood on your plan where its afternoon shadow will cool an otherwise very warm corner in summer.

At this stage of developing your design plan for plants, it would be a good idea to review which are perennials, biennials, and annuals. If you would rather skip this subject, then do not be surprised if a favorite plant of yours does not show up again next year. An annual simply disappears after one year unless it reseeds itself.

DAHLIA

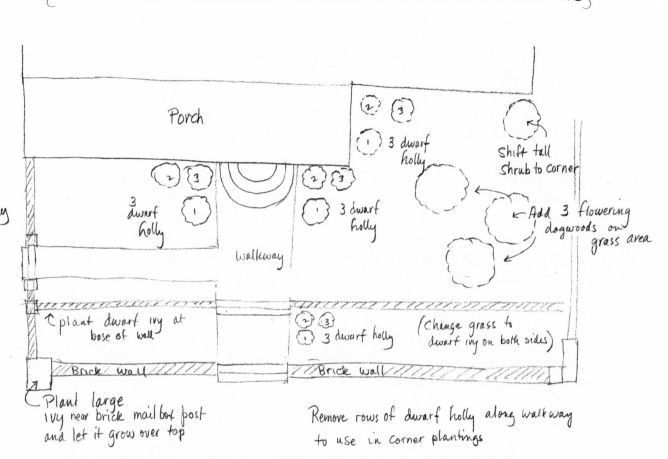

Porch

② ③

① 3 dwarf holly

Shift tall shrub to corner

Add 3 flowering dogwoods on grass area

② ③

3 dwarf holly

② ③

① 3 dwarf holly

walkway

↑ plant dwarf ivy at base of wall

② ③

① 3 dwarf holly

(Change grass to dwarf ivy on both sides)

Brick wall

Brick wall

↰ Plant large ivy near brick mailbox post and let it grow over top

Remove rows of dwarf holly along walkway to use in corner plantings

Your well-loved sweet William will do beautifully for two years and then die! It was meant to—it is a biennial. But you can always count on irises. They and other perennials have a life span of more than two seasons and will keep on indefinitely with care.

When putting down on paper the kinds of plants that will produce that beautiful garden you envision, care enough to find out their life expectancies—make sure that half of your materials do not disappear after the first year. Mother Nature is very smart indeed, and if you ask her for guidance, she will help you plant a garden that will bloom and bloom and bloom.

A vast majority of the most familiar flowers are annuals. These include zinnias, larkspurs, petunias, marigolds, etc. They bloom the first year they are planted, and then they die.

The biennials sprout the first year, bloom gloriously the second, and die the third year. Among this type are sweet Williams, Canterbury bells, foxgloves, and *Campanulas.*

The perennials become old friends you can depend on for many years. Irises, roses, chrysanthemums, dahlias, and gladioli are among the finest. Most perennials succumb finally because of bugs, lack of irrigation, or a frightful winter.

June is the time for you to plant the flowers in the plan by placing them in beds. Whether you are planting flowers in full bloom or with just roots, you put them in their exact locations according to color harmonies carefully worked out beforehand. After a gentle, thorough soaking, properly selected plants will be convinced that they have always lived there.

So remember, if the plan is developed with care and implemented in a timely fashion, the garden will be in full bloom for months before the first frost. And its personality will flourish as well.

The Magic of Night

A different world appears at night, one which seems to be composed of odd shapes and pale colors. The personalities of every landscape, each nook and cranny, are utterly changed; and fairies seem to have flown about leaving lighted candles at trees, water, and paths—much to the delight of us mere human beings who live here. Never forget the magic of night; design your plan to get the most out of it.

Remember that soft lighting features color at its best, with no object lost unless it should be obscured in darkness.

For the sake of experiment, choose a mild night and beginning at dusk attach a few light bulbs to long electric cords. Select a favorite plant with excellent structure such as a hemlock and illuminate it. Suffused with a soft glow, its beauty is fascinating.

Watch a tulip poplar's trunk turn into a silver shaft with silky branches against a black sky. Take one long, pink Oriental poppy and bring it out of total darkness with a stream of light, and there will emerge a strangely beautiful composition.

Be careful when actually installing your night lighting. Locate all wiring so that it will not be damaged by digging or pose a threat to curious children and animals. You will be rewarded with a dramatic night landscape.

You can count on several blooming plants to be real stars. The Golden Rain tree *(Laburnum)* is covered with yellow flowers in summer. *Chionanthus virginica,* wrapped in white shreds, resembles coconut in springtime and later produces butter-yellow foliage. Early Yoshino cherry presents white flowers with a pale pink glow, and pink Autumnalis cherry blooms late.

The white dogwoods and crabapples *(Malus floribunda)* are beautiful, steady bloomers with colorful autumn foliage. Just think how delightful it would be to drive through an allée of blooming trees!

Here I am repeating a word of caution: Never alternate single trees of different kinds. Always plant several of each variety together with spaces between groups.

Magnolias and hollies are stunning when bathed in night light. Also very special are the ethereally beautiful lines of graceful January jessamine *(Jasminum nudiflorum)* and Carolina yellow jessamine vines.

Colors such as purple, blue, dark brown, and dark green seem to swallow various tones and combinations and, as a result, are less spectacular at night. But notice the grays and whites! Leaves and flowers seem to be encased in ice and are enchanting. Boxes and pots full of such plants by doorways produce their own show, but be careful not to overdo this lovely effect. Quiet beauty is the finest result, so watch all combinations carefully or your hard work may produce something garish like fire-crackers let loose on New Year's Eve.

A plain, nondescript driveway has a chance to steal the show. First, line it with flowering trees, which can produce fabulous dividends in many ways. The display of springtime flowers will be followed by fresh, new green foliage that turns to brilliant colors in the fall. As the foliage disappears, the shapes and contours of limbs emerge and, when silhouetted, look for all the world like stunning pen-and-ink sketches.

JULY

Summer Struggles and Triumphs

What looks good in the heat? Not much. Where do you like to walk in the heat? Nowhere. So your pace slows up in the summer, and life must be uncluttered outside the house as well as in. At this time of year more than at any other, the large terrace, the spacious walk, the pool of shade count for real comfort. Narrow passages, crowded areas, and clutter only annoy. With a little imagination, create an open feeling, keep the air circulating, and make the yard cool and inviting.

First, tackle views from windows and doors, adjusting for the planned color and texture of each season to make sure there are not any gaps in the design plan. Start with the evergreens such as white-and-green pittosporum, cleyera, *Ilex convexa, Vinca minor,* and the evergreen trees. This material immediately creates a calm, cool, and serene setting. Then add annuals as you wish, although one allamanda in a tub, or six pots of pure white, miniature dahlias would be completely satisfying. Here, indeed, is the closest thing to no upkeep, yet beautiful in design.

There is no time like July to see mistakes in color groups and in quantities within flower borders. While plants are in full bloom, it is easy to count how many clumps there should have been and to appreciate how much more effective or pleasing a different color combination could be. You can also thoroughly enjoy your successes for they are apparent now or never.

This is the time to study your garden's background. It, too, will be at its best or at its worst. If it has seemed weak and ineffective since early spring, plan now for the future restructuring it needs. Walks or fences will be your greatest asset in displaying the garden to its best advantage, with well-pruned and well-fertilized shrubs a close second.

There is bloom all over the place during the month of July: *Rudbeckias* (black-eyed Susans) are there, *Mentha longifolia* (horsemint), *Platycodon,* hybrid daylilies, petunias and other low-foliage plants in profusion. With the results now before your eyes, you can see that it makes sense to plant high, medium, and low groups. You can see how beautiful stiff clumps of *Rudbeckia* are in the rear, how perfect *Stokesia* is in the middle, and how petunias and cushion chrysanthemums tie it all up in a neat package as the lowest masses in front.

RUDBECKIA

Even at the height of summer lushness it is surprising how often the small lot can seem more spacious than the large one. When space is limited, you must use every available inch to good advantage and think ideas through even more carefully before you act.

Will a tight planting space accommodate three raphiolepsis (an evergreen oriental shrub) or four? Is one small Bechtel crabapple tree the answer, or can you possibly get away with three Moraine locusts planted in a clump? Consider whether an entire four-foot-wide area should be surfaced with brown pebbles or brick for a walkway, but do not divide the small area further by making it part grass and part flagstone.

It is true that the small space or lot needs close attention to stay at its best. Sometimes a gardener can get very tired of pruning,

STOKESIA

but that once-a-week-inspection can keep plant material from getting out of hand. Put special emphasis now on ivy, Carolina yellow jessamine, pittosporum, boxleaf holly of all varieties, pyracantha, McArtney roses, and Burford hollies. The tedious work has its compensation in the great result when you mix well-pruned shrubs, trees, and vines. It is soul-satisfying when nothing is crowded and all plants are in good health.

Perhaps there is space for only one very small flower bed. If so, plant it with a mass of basically one flower, one color. You will discover that a four-by-ten foot strip of yellow tulips with a ground cover of apricot violas in spring, followed by pure white petunias for summer, followed in autumn by eight yellow cushion chrysanthemums is a pure joy. And weeds are completely outfoxed.

Let no one disparage the "small place," for its owner is sitting pretty. This is the place that gets hand care and loving and careful inspection, and every bloom and berry is enjoyed totally.

AJUGA

Consider just such a situation on one gardener's small lot. Although she inherited a good general layout, through sheer determination she persuaded each shrub, tree, and vine to keep its place and to grow as it had never grown before. When for the sake of a doorway half a pyracantha needed cutting out, she cut it. When a Burford holly encroached on the driveway, the shrub was promptly put in its place. A terrace—only fifteen feet in depth—was gouged out and surrounded by a very necessary retaining wall. It was built of broken octagonal sidewalk blocks—all in one day! Everything counts, everything shows on a small lot. Happy is the gardener who owns one.

Whether the space is small or large, one universal problem seems to be the care and planting of banks. There is bound to be some kind of a bank unless a lot is perfectly flat; and a two-foot-high bank that is carelessly planted is just as great a problem as one fifteen feet high. If it seems unnecessary to remind gardeners that flowing materials are essential for sloping areas, just look around. You see ugly, bare banks all too often.

Never feature banks, but grade and plant them to form smooth backgrounds. They can actually be useful in that respect. A slope in the shade or sun, covered with *Ajuga,* small-leaf ivy, or *Vinca minor* ceases to be a problem. Should there be some need to add interest to a shady slope, plant caladiums, coleus, or hosta at the top and bottom, but not on the slope itself. Cover the sloping face with your choice of dwarf evergreen material.

The most difficult situation of all is the high bank of fifteen to twenty feet in total or partial sun and in full view all the time. Ivy, planted with roots—

VINCA MINOR

not cuttings—and deeply mulched, does very well even in this sunny setting. Or you can cover the entire bank with *Polygonum reynoutria* (silver lace vine) that blooms in the hottest weather with pink flowers resembling blossoms of the coral vine. Another alternative is Carolina yellow jessamine, but if you are considering a substantial area of it, you should be aware that its flowers are poisonous.

Never forget that the first and basic requirement in coping with banks is a foolproof grading job. If the grading is done correctly, you can solve the other problems.

A Touch of Charm

We might as well face the fact that some houses are sturdy, strong, and homely. There will never be a leak, nor will there ever be any real charm unless we work to put it there. The house built foursquare to resist the elements could have been shifted slightly to take advantage of a distant woodland view, but that is hindsight. Yet, all is not lost; transformations are definitely possible.

Consider a bleak, square house with a roof jammed firmly on top like a sturdy felt hat. To soften such a situation there must be trees—their shadows deepen the tone of violent red brick and soften that determined-looking roof. For starters, create the illusion of trees by drawing them in on the design plan. Put a group of trees to the side of the house, with one or two placed alone toward the center. Include two or three evergreen Carolina hemlocks.

Remember that foliage may be a different color during the summer. There are bronzy greens of Hopa crabapple, purples of the purple-leaf plum, orange-red and chartreuse of Japanese cutleaf maple, and pale green of weeping willows. Particularly if you use a few carefully chosen colors, trees planted where they are badly needed can create a rich and beautiful effect.

HEMLOCK

You can get striking results with dwarf shrubs if you group them at strategic corners instead of lining them up and cutting square corners. Consider their ultimate height, for "dwarf shrub" does not mean that all varieties measure the same.

The right plant material, well placed and thoughtfully handled, will make up for what the house itself lacks in harmony and charm. There is no reason why a delightful view cannot be created where there is really a need for one. Study the yard from major windows and doors and decide what view you want to create. From each vantage point, contain the selected area by planting a thick background of favorite evergreens such as Carolina or Canadian hemlocks.

BARBERRY

Remember, a "view" does not necessarily mean distant hills. A very small shade tree by a small pool surrounded with flower beds and enclosed by beautiful fencing surely presents a fetching composition. Without it, you might have street intersections, a neighbor's garbage cans, or work areas. (By the way, have you stepped next door or across the street lately to see how your garbage cans look?)

Plant material that changes its appearance at different times of the year is fascinating if it is not needed for constant screening. For instance, Hopa crabapple changes completely from spring to summer to winter, offering more privacy some seasons than others. Summertime finds Julianne barberry covering itself with heavy yellow flowers, but fall has other plans, producing an abundance of red foliage as the yellow flowers fade away. *Photinia glabra* changes its dress from brilliant red in the spring to olive green for summer and winter.

Flowers change, too. Many gardeners think that zinnias, marigolds, and roses are far prettier in the fall than in spring and summer. The magnificent clematis blooms leave behind them an array of amusing shaggy heads.

Beauty always fills a need. It is natural to want a peaceful vista that includes no other house, no unsightly garage doors. There is a delightful sense of achievement in making each view more charming and more personal by adding small features. A small stone cat curls up on a low brick post; a few frogs look goggle-eyed into the pool; a large smooth stone balances several potted plants; a cast iron or concrete shell on the ground holds water for birds and rabbits. And there is not a pink flamingo in sight— peace and harmony!

The Elusive Focal Point

Selecting and placing a focal point is not easy, but a focal point is the key element of your design plan. We are talking about a stable object—such as a fountain, a bench, a piece of sculpture, or even a plant—that becomes the center of attention and toward which other elements point. Finding the ideal location takes study and trial and error. The focal point determines how a whole area will be seen, and once you work this out successfully, your total design will come alive.

The focal point may already be there, and all you have to do is take advantage of it. If not, be certain that the object you select is appropriate in its setting. For instance, you would not want to put a contemporary sculpture in the traditional yard of an old-fashioned house. If nothing like a bench, a statue, a sundial, or a fountain seems to work, turn to plant material—the simplest and most natural focal point of all.

A well-shaped, white-blooming crape myrtle on an oval pad of green-and-white ivy could be a stunning center of attention. Or the same white crape myrtle surrounded by late azaleas, weigelas, blue hydrangeas, and strawberry-pink burning bush would announce its seasonal climax with a burst of pure white. Snow in summer!

Especially beautiful focal points can be found in masses of the following plants: pink and rose-red azaleas planted together, fall-blooming cherry trees, a hillside of

TERRA COTTA RABBIT AMONG
THE HOSTA AND DWARF MONDO

Virginia bluebells, a large open area covered with the blue field pansy *(Viola kitaibelisana),* tall pink dahlias in a large group against a fence corner.

Foliage plants that provide greenery for Thanksgiving and Christmas decorations can make excellent focal points. The golden-tipped arborvitae is a great candidate, for instance, because of the impact of its fine tones and flat, fan-shaped foliage. At the same time, it is difficult to place outdoors because it requires a solid and subdued background. This eliminates varicolored bricks and deciduous shrubs as backdrops, but it is extremely handsome in front of solid green holly, ligustrums and osmanthus, dark chocolate brown or dark green fences, or soft pink brick.

The often-maligned Pfitzer juniper is the best possible supply source for wreaths and swags. Place it so it can joyfully grow to its complete seven-foot height without fuss. The Burford holly is ready to provide an endless supply of large green branches loaded with red berries. For use as a focal point it must be allowed to grow loose and long, clipped only seasonally for its festive bounty.

No foliage is richer as a center of attention than that of aucuba. Hunt for shade and plant a supply of the solid green and the variety named Gold Dust. (When decorating for the holidays, anise is delightful with aucuba in a large arrangement. Add fruit for a very satisfactory and bountiful result.)

The virtues of magnolia foliage cannot be overemphasized. Have one somewhere, for nothing takes its place.

Cryptomeria and Cunninghamia are beautiful as focal points and as cut greenery. Their scale is very large and their texture extremely handsome. It seems a pity that so few homes have adequate supplies of the finest broadleaf evergreens in an area where so many varieties grow to perfection. Let us spread the word.

AUGUST

Little Things Mean a Lot

Despite its heat, August is an intriguing month as the slow realization breaks all around you that shrubs and trees are still full of rich growth. They are ready and willing to form a delightful background for the colorful walks into cooler September.

Notice the details: vines growing up a lamp post at the front door, bright flowers growing along walks from car to kitchen door, a group of dwarf hollies clustered by the brick steps. Do not sell August short.

Thick vines of small-leaf ivy at the door reward close scrutiny. Touched by the heavenly perfume of the honeysuckle from a nearby fence, you suddenly recognize that the pale pink draperies in the dining room are in harmony with soft pink tones of Amsonia in flower beds below the windows. It is all a delightful composition.

That short gravel walk to the kitchen door can be transformed if you cover it with carefully cut squares of soft gray slate. It will be beautiful, and it will keep the sharp gravel out of your shoes.

Consider planting groups of zinnias in solid colors on each side of the walk. There are stunning new sizes and colors in the varieties developed recently. Back up the zinnia groups with pittosporum or guava or both. Aucuba foliage with pittosporum and mahonia planted near one another in separate groups form a fine trio, and selected laurels with various yews are a delight.

Weeds, bermuda grass, and summer rains go together, and, unfortunately, weeds and grass always grow abundantly in the wrong places. So begin outwitting them for the rest of the summer and next year. When weeds sprout through joints in walks or terrace areas, they can be sprayed or pulled.

On the edges of terraces or walks, use bands of ivy or flowers, and outline them with metal or brick edging to make weed pests keep their distance. If neither ivy nor flowers are feasible, the metal or brick edges alone can handle the situation very well. The more distance weeds must travel, the better.

Often, long flower beds seem to be engulfed overnight with a sea of weeds. This usually happens because there are not enough vigorous flowers in the bed, and weeds can march in and gobble up all available space. Large masses of sturdy, single petunias, zinnias, or hybrid daylilies do not leave much room for bermuda grass or weeds to establish their roots. Full, thick cultivation is the answer here.

Around shrubs, you can weed with greater ease if the heavy plants are not packed too closely together. Where shrubs are crowded, their branches become entwined and make it impossible to climb among them to do any weeding or cleaning. You can create barriers by laying twelve-inch-wide strips of bricks flat along the borders of shrub beds. The bricks can be sprayed if necessary, and you will be successful in keeping weeds and grass at a distance.

Just do not leave too much uncultivated space in any planted beds. Keep shrub planting simple, and keep the sand joints of edgings at a minimum. Those weeds will be put in their place to stay.

Ups and Downs

Differences in levels create intriguing problems. There are so many ways to get up or down that it is always best to experiment on paper before you decide on any one approach. Take this chance to be creative. You could work with stones, originally designed ironwork, a creative brick pattern, or fine-colored concrete.

Available space has a great deal to do with a solution. Smoothly sloping banks feathered out into existing grades are restful where there is plenty of room. But when every foot is needed for daily walking, gardening, or sitting, a retaining wall, no matter how rough, can be your best friend. It not only gives you every available inch, but such a wall could also become the back of a tool house or hot house.

Sloping land on small lots wastes crucial space. It may be covered with attractive plants, but it cannot be used for play, walking, or gardening. Remember that necessary walls need not be straight with square corners; they can curve, becoming one of the finest flowing lines on the entire lot. They can also handle their grade by becoming wide, beautiful steps as they drop or climb.

Planted pockets on steps often are more successful than those tucked into walls. The step pockets on treads are flat, while those in walls are sheer or sloping. Where plant materials such as *Teucrium,* lemon verbena, sedums of all kinds, cheddar pinks, portulaca, *Euonymus radicans* (shade), *Santolina,* and *Torenia* (shade) are gathered into a rich, handsome group, the wall designed as planted steps may become the focal point of the entire garden.

A friend has done just this. She has wrapped her fine contemporary home around a spacious terrace. The view through her glass walls flows across sixty feet of curving steps that form a necessary retaining wall. This marvelous piece of design provides a completely satisfying visual experience any time of the year.

RETAINING WALL PLANTED WITH SEDUM

Quality construction is the key to such successful solutions. Then, with the help of a few well-placed trees and shrubs, the composition holds its own in any weather, in any season. Up or down, make the transition beautiful and it can be the backbone, the final touch, the climax of your delightful home and garden.

The Wild Ones—The Tame Ones

Plants that seem to appear of their own free will are often the most charming, the most interesting and delightful in our horticultural world. For instance, the tiny ground cover known as boxweed simply appears in shady, damp corners and proceeds to spread anywhere there is space. The results are gratifying—lovely to look at, no cost, no upkeep.

Woodland ferns of many kinds are as interesting as any variety you can buy. Their uses are legion, and left to their own devices they respond with astonishing, abundant growth. Stream banks held with a combination of stones, ferns, forget-me-nots, and dwarf daylilies do not collapse but become even more attractive with time.

Who has ever seen a wild azalea in the "wrong" place? These exquisite plants provide natural form to otherwise monotonous bland areas, and they like the company of butterfly weed, ferns, bee balm, and Indian Paint Brush. The way natural growth appears is constantly intriguing: one plant simply occurs; then from this source come others until a colony is formed. One root will then detach itself, acting as a sort of advance scout, sprouting alone many yards ahead. It creates another colony.

Nature has its own way of contrasting various sizes and shapes of foliage. *Magnolia glauca,* aralia, leucothoe, and sumac provide a visual delight that teaches several things: One old plant and several young ones balance each other, and high and low groups are twice as interesting as plants of one size.

WHO HAS EVER SEEN A WILD AZALEA IN THE "WRONG" PLACE?

The beauty of summer trees is astonishing: sourwoods form brilliant clumps, with rarely a single straight trunk; pin oaks are as symmetrical as if they were just lately measured and sheared. The majestic grandeur of one native beech calls for a bench nearby so you can feast your eyes on branch structure alone.

What greater joy is there than being surrounded with magnificent native plant material that has cared for itself for years? Guard these wild ones, large or small, for they are one of your finest investments.

August is especially rich in interesting colors, shapes, and sizes throughout the garden. Look around you now to determine just how successful your design plan is at the height of summer growth. Make notes, listing the best results in all areas as well as ideas for improvements. The bounty of this month will carry you all the way into late September.

Superb color and form in dwarf and regular crape myrtles make a special contribution: the dwarfs create rich masses of color much as large azaleas do, and the taller species are striking as slender trees. The most important point to remember is to group colors, never alternate them.

Seed pods on Golden Rain trees provide striking and decorative formations now and into September. Quick shade and fine texture are also good attributes of these trees.

The large shrubby mallows in vivid colors, from white with red centers through solid burgundy, are perfect for morning effect (they close in the afternoon). Use them in wide open spaces near lakes, in front of magnolias, viewed beyond swimming pools, across large lawns, near walkways and sitting areas.

Cannas are spectacular now, with their stately air and magnificent colors. Consider the new dwarf varieties in shrimp pink and yellow. Always plant cannas in groups, never in lines.

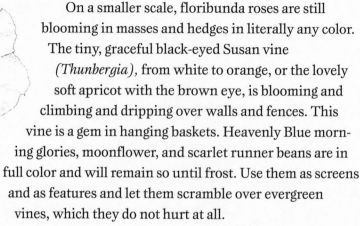

MOONFLOWER

On a smaller scale, floribunda roses are still blooming in masses and hedges in literally any color. The tiny, graceful black-eyed Susan vine *(Thunbergia),* from white to orange, or the lovely soft apricot with the brown eye, is blooming and climbing and dripping over walls and fences. This vine is a gem in hanging baskets. Heavenly Blue morning glories, moonflower, and scarlet runner beans are in full color and will remain so until frost. Use them as screens and as features and let them scramble over evergreen vines, which they do not hurt at all.

Backing up all of this exotic summer color is a world of fine evergreens. The dwarf *Osmanthus heterophyllus,* the spruce, the *Ilex aquifolium* are among many striking evergreen beauties. Here is character. We need no "fillers" in our plans.

Subdivision Entrances and Amenities

Have you noticed your own subdivision lately? Actually close up? If you are fortunate, each owner really seems to care, which is not only a blessing for you, but also very important to the entire neighborhood and to property values as a whole.

Even before developers sell lots, the best of them are meticulous concerning details of planning and planting. There is a farsighted use of basic evergreen shrubs and ground covers and carefully chosen varieties of trees. Such planning ahead means that later, when homeowners assume responsibilities for upkeep, all plants will have a healthy head start.

Quality landscaping adds beauty and value to your subdivision, and there are certain guidelines that are well worth following to maintain these advantages. First, continue to use evergreen plant material throughout the neighborhood, adding seasonal blooming material where there is adequate space and water. Next, do not allow tall shrubs and trees to be planted in any location where their growth might restrict the views of vehicular traffic or encroach on utility lines.

Third, purchase only the finest, cleanest plants to emphasize exits, entrances, and special focal points. Select them carefully. When picking tall evergreens, for instance, consider Carolina hemlocks for they are sturdy and beautiful throughout the entire year.

Black-green podocarpus, cephalotaxus, boxwood, and miniature or large ivy form stunning compositions with red brick or cream brick houses. When different colors are present on clapboard houses—such as white siding, brown gables, and green shutters—the last thing to use is any kind of variegated plant material. Hold to solid greens and add interest by introducing different shapes and sizes—from *Osmanthus fortunei* to cotoneaster, on to cleyera. All of these plants are different, rich, and beautiful.

There is an endless amount of fine plant material available. The problem is keeping your enthusiasm within bounds. Do not plant one of something unless there is that perfect spot for one completely developed specimen plant such as a Carolina or Canadian hemlock. As a rule, plant in groups of twos or threes.

Remember that the most harmonious result will come from a detailed design plan for the entire subdivision. Attention to landscape amenities will help to inspire all owners to cherish the balance, proportion, and beauty of their own entrances, driveways, gardens, and front and back yards.

Go across the street, turn, and give your own house and lot a long, careful look. That good feeling of accomplishment is worth every minute of planning ahead. No part of nature is ever final, so prepare yourself for an incomparable journey.

$\mathcal{S}$UMMER $\mathcal{C}$HORES

JUNE: The month to take a good look at your trees. Remember that the instructions for watering trees in the southern zones are different from the northern and western areas, so check your source. Be aware of the cadence of wind, rain, and sun in your area and the effect it has on the trees, then water accordingly. One rule holds true no matter what section of the country you live in: all new trees, set out for less than two years, need slow soaking.

June is a good month to do a little "housecleaning" by pruning dead ends from tree limbs and removing shriveled foliage from shrubs. Evergreen trees can be pruned if necessary. Dead wood is easy to see now that a year's growth has already been acccomplished.

This is also the month for pinching back newly planted annuals and for cutting or brushing off shriveled blooms from rhododendrons, azaleas, and laurel. After daffodil foliage has turned yellow, the bulbs can be moved or separated if necessary, or you can keep them where they are and braid their foliage for neatness.

A wisteria that refuses to bloom must have its runners as well as its roots cut back severely. Do not hurry: take your time and do a thorough job. While colors and textures are at their peak, be critical of every plant so that each can be displayed to its best advantage. Discover the amazing beauty of new zinnia varieties and plant those seeds now. They will be a lovely sight, and there will be plenty for cutting into November.

JULY: The month for watering. The most important job out of doors now is to follow a watering and soaking schedule. Very small plants revel in being watered slowly—by soaking—since their size can rarely handle a huge drink all at once. The job is slow and tiresome, but if you mulch carefully with pine straw or pine pellets or dead leaves after watering, you will not have to water again so soon. Secure an estimate from a local irriga-tion contractor, or check out do-it-yourself irrigation systems. However you water, it is a necessary and worthwhile investment.

Pinch dahlias and chrysanthemums back so there will be plenty of blooms in the fall. Divide old irises and plant some of the new bearded varieties.

AUGUST: A sturdy, busy month producing good results with whatever plants were started in June and July. Take cuttings of your favorite phlox and snapdragons, and divide Japanese irises. Give those chrysanthemums and dahlias a light monthly feeding, stopping as buds begin to show color. For steady growth and fine bloom, use a complete plant food such as 8-8-8.

August never looks like the last of anything, for it is bulging with colorful cosmos, marigolds, zinnias, celosia, and healthy lawns. Just keep dead blooms off of all plants, and water and fertilize the heavy feeders. Then August will push into September with vigor, giving us plenty to anticipate from fall.

JAPANESE MAPLE

Fall

September · October · November

September is a neatly packaged month that invites you to perform certain rituals. Take slow walks around your property, carefully studying the growth of spring and summer. Fall has a way of revealing deficiencies very quickly. Some shrubs and trees have developed well and seem to be ready for whatever the weather has to offer. This is heartening, for after September and October, November closes the door.

September carries off the transition from summer to fall with its own special flair. The first autumn leaf color seems cleaner and brighter than ever before. Chrysanthemum blooms are fresh and intense, and celosias and cleome continue to enjoy being alive. The first inkling of autumn is revealed by the blood-red sourwoods that beat October to the wire by a few weeks.

Perennial asters are carrying on in flower borders as if frost were unknown, and small single dahlias are in full bloom. Masses of floribunda roses and fall-blooming crocuses are having a wonderful time. If you plant these crocuses in wooded areas and even in zoysia-planted areas, you will have a blanket of purple and gold to enjoy for several weeks.

This is a splendid month for tree planting, so add a hickory and ginkgo if there is room. And "room" means twelve to fifteen feet apart, for both of these butter-yellow trees must be allowed to grow slowly in order to show their lovely outlines.

Bring out your plan notebook and list the following plants to put in next spring, and you will have beautiful falls in the future:

FALL
BLOOMING
CROCUS

- Small yellow marigolds
- White and pale pink midget zinnias
- Rosemary
- Green-and-gray *Santolina*
- Yellow and pink celosia
- Fall-blooming crocuses
- Perennial asters
- Single small dahlias
- Purple-and-white sweet alyssum (blooms into late October)
- *Alternanthera* (Joseph's Coat—brilliant foliage)
- *Polygonum reynoutria* in beautiful frothy pink
- Cushion chrysanthemums.

Striking among shrubs, the completely scarlet brook euonymus or burning bush (*Euonymus alatus*) is beginning to smolder in early September. Add several wintersweet shrubs *(Meratia praecox)* and eleagnus, and be ready for a very fragrant October.

For impact, add cushion chrysanthemums that are approaching their height of bloom. And if you throw in flaming red pigmy barberry, a small sensation will be in the making.

Speaking of color, do not give up on color if parts of your yard are in deep shade. There are dozens of available plants such as varicolored hosta, fern, hardy astilbe, caladium, and even lily of the valley. Have high expectations, and go ahead with some spring planting now if weather is mild.

October is show time for trees. Silhouettes of Bradford pears, maple, beech, gingko, and crabapple are constant marvels. Feast the eye and calm the soul in the fall and early winter with groups of these beauties close by.

Consider developing attractive, open family space where one can turn the chairs around for special use: watching the bird feeders, listening to a small waterfall, enjoying the evergreen Carolina yellow jessamine vines nearby. These vines are soothing to the touch, and they might be arranged so that they frame a superb view of the sunset.

November can have dramatic impact just by avoiding that bare and colorless look which cold weather often brings. Rich and lustrous magnolias always shine in the sun, and the many exquisite varieties of ivy can be counted on to warm white stone walls with thick, green, ornamental cascades.

All growing things are ready now for a little rest. During this dormant period, before January can begin another growing year, remember that design must be your first consideration. The miraculous change of the seasons is given to us, but we cannot make the most of nature unless we put sound design elements in place.

No matter how much planting is changed, added, or taken up, results are not going to be improved if the basic design is crudely done or completely wrong. A small walk will remain too narrow even though priceless dwarf evergreens are clustered along its edge. A bumpy, uneven terrace will continue to cause trouble even if surrounded by exquisite specimen roses.

Excellent planting can soften mistakes and lead the eye away from obvious errors, but it cannot correct the bad impression one always gets from the failure of basic design. If the proportion and balance are not right, if materials and grades have been wrong from the beginning, if there are no focal points to organize your perception of the landscape, then you must go back and tear out the design and start over again. Only then will fine planting, carefully chosen, fall into place comfortably like the pieces of an easy puzzle.

Why struggle to create a charming new flower border against a background of shrubs so large that they are grotesque? Why espalier lovely plants against a hideous wall? A good basic design plan will anticipate and help you avoid these problems and be an excellent long-term investment. Even the lowly zinnia looks queenly in a soul-satisfying setting, and one flowering tree will shine like a jewel on a well-graded lawn.

Have the courage to face up to the materials and perspectives that confront you and set things to rights once and for all. Then, and only then, can you enjoy using the wealth of colorful material that surrounds us.

If the basic design is right, three-fourths of the battle is won already.

SEPTEMBER

Unexpected Delight

Want to create more space, more color, more happiness and lasting beauty than ever seemed possible before? You can do it with design, well planned and thoughtfully developed. Orderliness, arrived at casually, can be so unobtrusive that it does not irritate, and herein lies the correct use of design.

"Design" does not mean always squaring things up, always outlining planting beds, always balancing shrub groups, always training loquats up walls. Such endless detail is enough to make one long for any kind of casual planting.

There is beauty and satisfaction in casual arrangements, even in the smallest spaces. Three low shrubs can balance one tall one perfectly. A curving path of blue stone, especially chosen, will get you to the gate with real beauty and just as fast as a rigid straight walk of precast stepping stones. A weeping willow on one side, actually pruned to fit if necessary, will soften any hard, ugly corner that may have heretofore belonged to the garbage can alone.

A few spots of long-lasting color carefully placed in a three-by-five foot area will hold their own, season after season, without any frantic redoing. Five pots of tulips—

CURVED WALKWAY LEADING TO GATE

three or more bulbs to a pot—can be sunk into the ground in the fall and dug up, intact, in late spring after they bloom. In this same area there can be three clumps of sturdy, handsome *Rudbeckia* that will start blooming the first of May and continue, no doubt, until frost. These spots of color are ideal, of course, as the view framed by your favorite window—a kind of veiled orderliness that is the indispensable tool of good design and is never tiresome.

Plan for the unexpected delight. Develop a secluded corner of approximately twelve by fifteen feet as an enclosed sitting area. Feature one crabapple tree with an undercover of bronze *Ajuga*. Fill in with one dwarf Chinese holly, two *Ilex helleri,* one Carolina yellow jessamine vine, several white caladiums, a dark green fence and gate, and a gray flagstone floor. Claim your own charming space and defy anyone to occupy your chair in the midst of it!

If there is a handy faucet, build a tiny pool there to hold one water lily. Put a *Daphne odora* nearby—in a large clay pot if ground space is tight. Now select cushion chrysanthemums and only those broadleaf evergreens that delight your eye. There is small weeping *Lonicera* (shrub honeysuckle) for drooping over the wall, podocarpus for training straight up against the house, and dichondra seeds to poke down in between bricks and stones on the ground.

Before you plant a little bit of everything, be sure that there is enough open flat area for your one chaise or comfortable waterproof chair. To be a complete success you want the whole composition to look best from a prone position!

Do construction and clearing out first and your planting second. Avoid clutter like a fungus. When you are ready, put in a few shrubs any time during winter in open weather. Do not forget to plant at least one mass of tulips close by. Then get set for a bit of well-deserved enjoyment from your design efforts.

The Major Addition

The design plan is stretching in several different directions now. The latest addition could be a pool or a deck or a patio or a greenhouse, or whatever is *your* next step.

Let us say you have dreamed of a greenhouse for many years, and now it is really there. You are ready to celebrate, but somehow there is a problem. A walkway must be laid to the greenhouse. Where in the world are you going to put it? To get to the greenhouse you must walk clear around the house! Why wasn't it planned to incorporate the side door?

Maybe a pool has been the big project for the future, and now you are ready to tackle it. Measuring and planning for a pool can go on for hours—and should. This will be an all-absorbing process. The secret of completing the project successfully and creating a pool that is a harmonious part of your overall design is careful and thorough planning.

Too often you actually get the financing for the pool unexpectedly, and there is just barely time to get it built before summer. Planning is sketchy. Construction, for once, is smooth and uneventful. Everything is on schedule; the pool will be ready when school is out!

The first day of vacation dawns bright and sunny. The pool is finished, the water is in, and the whole family goes swimming for the first time. Oh, no! All you see from the pool are the open underpinnings of your house. Not only does the house seem to be on stilts, it has all of the utilities plus garbage cans lined up in military formation across the back.

Now, a kind of patch-up designing job must be done under pressure. If the pool and its setting had been developed on paper first, as an addition to your design plan, this disappointment could have been avoided. Take your time now and be especially thoughtful, for the job can be accomplished. It will be a little more difficult, but it can be done.

You work the design out by building a deck with trellis walls and wooden benches with backs. Your brand new view from the pool is a composition of deck and arbor, with raised planting pockets that will prevent the chlorinated water from splashing in and turning the soil a ghastly green.

The picture is peaceful from any angle, and the vista is lovely. The pool and its setting will be a joy for many years.

Those Extra Touches

Trellises and arbors have been a part of gardening design for centuries. Their use was fully recorded in early design books, and they still have a very definite place in vegetable and flower gardens today.

The adaptability of arbors enables us to use them as open roofs over hot terraces or decks. With the addition of beautiful vines, they create lush, leafy effects overhead. Hanging baskets of fuchsias and tuberous begonias seem to drip their colors everywhere and are a delightful addition to the summer scene.

Arbors for grapes and climbing tomatoes add fine details and background to vegetable gardens, which, in spite of their seasonal growth, are at times far more interesting than flower gardens. Try your hand at creating an arbor of small, trained fruit trees such as Bradford pears or flowering trees like white redbuds. The result of this training is known, in gardening terms, as pleached allées.

Trellises were never meant to be fragile, shiny white strips valiantly trying to support wildly uncontrollable climbing plant material. They are meant to be sturdy, well-designed panels for outdoor screening of breezeway, porch, carport, or arbor. They can provide ample support for a lovely mixture of seasonal vines, roses, or tomatoes, or for one handsome espalier. However simple, trellises should be well constructed and painted to blend with the entire design plan.

Just as arbors and trellises offer extra planting opportunities, the space beneath lightweight deciduous and evergreen trees and shrubs sometimes invites additional planting. Underplanting is the term that describes the process of adding low-growing material to these open areas.

Large-scale underplanting, by adding weight, color, and interest, can be much more effective than leaving a space in grass. Add a sweep of one color of low-growing azaleas under trees, for instance, or an evergreen covering of ivy, liriope, dwarf mondo, or *Vinca minor.* There are many other adaptable materials, but they must take semi-shade and should not defeat the original purpose of the design plan—that the trees remain the chief point of interest.

Any well-designed and well-cared-for underplanting keeps weeds at an absolute minimum and completely eliminates grass, making this a low-maintenance approach to long-term beauty. The older the plants become, the less care they need, which is the whole idea. The important facts to remember are that successful underplanting holds seasons together, gives continuity to the complete design plan, and holds moisture in the soil, while never outdoing the material above it.

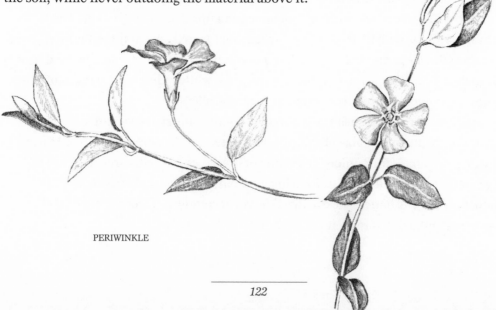

PERIWINKLE

OCTOBER

Pitfalls and Solutions

Beautiful October never quite prepares us for chilly November and December. Beguiling colorful trees in the glory of autumn mask our view of approaching bare branches and desolate strips of garden swept by cold winds. Some preparation can ward off upcoming dreary scenes, however.

Think of changeable weather as a rather difficult guest who will arrive, stay a while, raise certain challenges, and then leave. Get ready and hold onto the assurance that satisfying shapes and textures will prevail.

Clean up for your visitor. Begin by removing all the pots, which have been filled with colorful plants all summer, from decks, terraces, and entrances. If there are window boxes, replant them with pansies to provide a warmth that will carry over into springtime.

Nothing looks more frigid in chilly weather than outdoor metal chairs. Hustle them away and enjoy the extra open space—clean and clear.

Keep a critical eye on deciduous trees and shrubs during this transition time. Note dead wood or branches crossing and rubbing each other raw. Removing these is easy now, but difficult with heavy foliage. Taking the extra time and care in autumn will result in profuse blooming and healthier plants next spring.

WINDOW BOX
WITH PANSIES

Changing weather can reveal the strangest situations. For instance, how did those isolated, single, deciduous shrubs escape notice before? Surely they would appear to be more comfortable in groups, for one alone is a dreary sight. Take the initiative and add three or five evergreen Julianne barberry plants with blue berries and *Osmanthus fragrans* with perfumed white flowers. At the base of the shrubs plant autumn-flowering crocuses.

Group hollies laden with red berries here, and add purple-berried mahonias over there. Then no area need appear abandoned at any time during the winter months.

At this moment, how much evergreen material is accenting corners and turns in flower beds? Or do you just not walk that way in winter? A green garden design can actually take over the winter months with its own act—there is no need for desolation.

Dwarf boxwoods and dwarf hollies (and there are six or eight varieties of these) are essentially freeze-proof and need no pruning. The same is true of dwarf azaleas. The azaleas can also do the vital job of pointing up entrances and exits, enhancing a fine design plan.

Bare concrete or granite walls behind flower beds seem to be in a deep freeze as cold weather takes over, but evergreen vines come to the rescue. You can create needed warmth and color with loops or cascades of southern smilax or ivy or cotoneaster (not a vine, but most obliging) that drape over and hang down from the top of that grim wall. Or, espaliered *Camellia sasanqua* will change the mood of the scene for the better.

BARBERRY

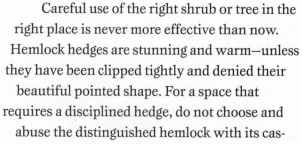

GINKGO

Careful use of the right shrub or tree in the right place is never more effective than now. Hemlock hedges are stunning and warm—unless they have been clipped tightly and denied their beautiful pointed shape. For a space that requires a disciplined hedge, do not choose and abuse the distinguished hemlock with its cascading branches and sharp point at the top. Choose a substitute: boxwood, Burford holly, ligustrum, photinia, pieris, mahonia, or barberry—to name but a few!

Often an area is so well balanced that it needs only one special something for a center of interest; then the area should be left alone. One carefully chosen tree, large or small depending on the size of the area, usually does the job neatly. A deciduous tree changes from season to season, becoming a fine winter etching. An evergreen might be more appropriate if you need a stable year-round center of interest.

There are any number of intriguing possibilities. Remember the deciduous ginkgo—that marvelous relic from prehistoric times—covered with golden, fan-shaped foliage in autumn. For a small selection, picture the beautifully constructed crabapple.

An evergreen? The blue spruce would be a strong accent in an empty spot. A group of dwarf magnolias, or only one, would be a striking relief in a dull, tight corner. Magnolias provide more than incomparable foliage and their huge white flowers. Make a note to discover the stunning purple collar that remains after the blooms have faded—beautiful in fall and winter arrangements!

Very few people are satisfied with their present grass, so how about a substitute? Dwarf mondo, for instance. It is flat, evergreen, good looking, easy to walk on, and never needs mowing. It grows well in sun or semishade. If half-sun and half-shade is what you have, plan for white- or lavender-flowering *Vinca minor,* adding a few stepping stones through it for convenience.

Since every detail outside is now in sharp focus, take a good look at your flower-bed edgings. Are they the strong, neat, attractive framework they should be? Or do they wobble off down the hill, mercifully disappearing? Many a design plan's success depends on carefully executed edgings, for without them the plan quickly unravels.

BRICK EDGING

There is a great difference between a single vertical brick edging and an edging using two bricks. The former is no real barrier to plant material on either side of it; plus it complicates mowing. The latter holds the detail of the design plan exactly as it should and gives a stable, flat trim for the power mower to zip along, cutting the grass evenly and safely.

Construct the double-brick edging with one-half of a vertical brick in the ground and one-half out of the ground. In front of that, full length forward, place another brick flat and flush to the ground. No mortar is necessary. Now, soil is not lost and plants do not deteriorate and die. Well-constructed edgings are worth the time.

Flagstone edging is possible, but it is more expensive since each piece must be cut. Also, the edges are very sharp and require extra caution when you work around them. Concrete outlines seem hard and unyielding, and concrete blends with nothing unless carefully colored. Wood strips rot, and you must use an edger for an even cut.

Fine detail in the execution of your design plan requires careful placement and grading. You must make wise choices in construction and plant material—from annuals and perennials to evergreens and vines—to insure that the result will give you pleasure for years.

Traffic Patterns

Circulation patterns of traffic have fascinated people for centuries. Massive steps and roads uncovered in ruins testify to the fact that getting there and back again has always been most important in the lives of people everywhere.

To hold a fine pattern—within a city or within a yard—where people can move with ease means that walls, steps, drainage, parking areas, trails, fences, and gates must be planned carefully, preferably before anyone sets foot in the area. Sometimes barriers will be necessary, although often there is only a need for well-placed groups of shrubs and trees to direct any number of people to their destination.

Beware of the no-thought, hit-or-miss layout. You are apt to find yourself stranded in an open area with no path or direction of any kind. When this happens, retaliate by taking the shortest distance between two points!

Well-designed walks and gates, easy to find, with a minimum width of four feet, announce that visitors are welcome here. A front door can be completely hidden around the wing of a house, but it is found with ease when a tall lantern surrounded with flowers points the way at the turn of an inviting walk.

Have you a few minutes of extra time this morning or afternoon or early evening? Any little pocket of time with daylight in it? If so, check out everything, get out the notebook, and do a little planning. There are things to be done that will have a memorable effect.

DAHLIA

First: Under that group of existing dogwoods, plant drifts of crocuses and daffodils. Or naturalize whole areas in white crocuses and white Mount Hood daffodils.

Second: Look into the mysteries of annuals, biennials, and perennials, even though development will be on a small scale. Get ready! Your own *Nicotiana* will bloom and smell sweetly at night, and a hummingbird will hover over spires of white salvia. Lose yourself in the wonder of the extra pockets of spare time; don't put things off until you have a whole day or weekend.

October is a wonderful month to survey all of your flowering materials. Spend an hour making three lists: one for the year's successes, one for failures, and one for new plants you have seen in other gardens and wish you had planted. Save the last one to consider in November, but work on the successes and failures.

Begin removing the failures (then there will surely be more room for successes and plants from your "wish list"). Examine the perennials that have done well. Add some breathing room among those that are too close together. Other plants, such as hostas, daylilies, and irises may need dividing. As you update your beds, be sure to bring your notebook up to date, too. Remember, your design plan need not be a masterpiece, just clear and workable.

The last job: Cut back tired plants and feed them lightly. Remove the top growth of such biennials as snapdragons.

Since this entire process is a learning experience, jot down the annuals, biennials, and perennials now in the garden. This reckoning will remind you of which is which (check on any you don't know). Remember, some will disappear and some remain.

While you are out taking care of October tasks, enjoy October's blooms. Chrysanthemums, celosia, and marigolds are more beautiful in this month than in any other. Phlox, also. Zinnias and large and small dahlias seem to show their deepest colors now. If you have some glaring empty spaces, buy a few such annuals and perennials already in bloom, slip them in, and have one glorious autumn.

ZINNIA

Church and Synagogue Grounds

From the Garden of Eden to the "lilies of the field," scripture offers ample praise of the outdoor world around us and ample inspiration to pay attention to landscape settings. Certainly no church or synagogue should sit by itself with no color, no evergreen ground cover, no trees. Such a setting shows an unfortunate lack of interest on the part of a congregation.

Our places of worship come in many sizes, shapes, and colors and a diversity of grounds. There is a great need of trees, shrubs, vines, and ground covers, and there is no one location within a church area where plants of any particular kind must go. Carefully designed and thoughtfully maintained grounds and gardens around synagogues and churches are an absolute joy any time of the year.

Following a few simple rules and using our same systematic design plan will help you get started. Study your church or synagogue from a distance. Remember that high evergreen material should be grouped at outside corners, medium-height evergreens go in the middle, and low-growing evergreens mark each side of front entrances.

Usually the front of such a building needs only a few evergreens, carefully chosen. You do not want to block out fine architectural details. If such details are lacking, then by all means add beauty and interest with additional broadleaf evergreen plant material. A delightful shape and fine foliage are the "musts." Whether or not plants bloom is optional; it is balance and proportion in combination with the design of the building that is important.

Do not, as a rule, put annual or perennial flower beds in front of the building. These materials should be confined to the "inside" gardens—spaces usually in back or in nooks of the building—used by congregation members. Each such garden should have a design plan. One area might be used for outdoor gatherings; another as a quiet corner to sit alone.

These planted areas will last for many happy years, so do not forget to provide for their maintenance and upkeep once they are established. If possible, build in an irrigation system. Have an annual budget and a committee of dedicated volunteer gardeners who will tend the gardens and grounds weekly.

One further suggestion: Consider a consultation with a landscape architect. Synagogues and churches are essentially public buildings, with larger constituencies to be satisfied and larger areas to be planned than an individual home and lot. Even an hour or two with a landscape professional can provide a simple, permanent, workable plan that will get the congregation started in a sound direction.

BURFORD HOLLY

NOVEMBER

Weather Changes

November arrives—a shock even though it comes every year and we know it must follow the mellow glories of September and October. The thoughtful planning you have done all year—and continue to do—makes it easier to accept the weather changes.

Life flows on in thousands of engaging shapes and textures. Do not disrupt the quiet elegance of broadleaf evergreens such as hollies and magnolias with chimes that ring or clatter in the breeze. Appreciate the thick, green dwarf mondo or other ground covers as they refuse to allow the cold winds to desolate your garden.

Surprise yourself by sowing larkspur and cornflower seeds in available flower bed openings, for they will be a beautiful sight in late spring. Add new plants of shasta daisies, sweet William, and coreopsis in empty places. Sweet peas on a trellis—try it! Plant tulip bulbs if you are sure there are no moles in that area, and add fresh topsoil to beds where needed.

At no time need there be a blank spot in your garden area. Tall groups of *Sarcococca* in beds surrounded by edgings of silver-gray *Santolina* are handsome with a ground cover of hellebore (Christmas rose) to bloom in December.

The standard Foster hollies, obelisks of *Ligustrum coriaseum,* and balls of ivy are now the main characters in a winter play, and how beautifully do they interpret their parts. They are sentinels at entrances or accents all the way down center lines of beds or focal points against walls or fences. Five or six of one kind grouped in the center of a paved terrace area delight the eye from breakfast room, kitchen, library. All winter they present a picture of warm beauty.

Dark, glossy green smilax vines in shady areas continue to act as flowing draperies in winter as they do in summer. Giving a form and richness to shade—which shade needs—the vines ask only for an adequate trellis. They do the rest.

Add a few evergreen cherry laurel trees, short-needle pines, yaupon hollies, Japanese oaks, and large Burford hollies pruned as trees, and you wonder why anyone need look at a deserted and abandoned landscape at any time.

As beautiful as the bone structures of cherries, crabapples, and dogwoods are, why not combine their etching with the green? When one really explores the possibilities of green gardens and their winter worth, there is no turning back. They will surround you with warm beauty and escort you triumphantly through winter and into spring.

SOUTHERN
SMILAX

Green Winter Gardens

You can actually go beyond the evergreen foundations that soften the winter landscape and create green winter gardens. To assure good results you must take logical steps in sequence and use a bit of imagination, but once it's done it stays done—an unusually fine dividend.

Locate the garden in an area that makes sense, not at the end of the garage or outside the bathroom window just because these spots are level. Be sure you create a view from a living area. You may even echo color from inside to outside.

Stake out a good location, laying off beds carefully with neatly set bricks, cut stones, or treated wood edgings. If you use wood, remember that it must eventually be replaced.

Next, look to the surface color of paths and beds. The very best time to make this selection is during cold, gray, forbidding days. If the combination of shredded brown pine bark and rich gray flagstone with clipped evergreen edges is beautiful now, it will warm the heart any time.

Check the layout from your viewing area as you progress. Realize that paths can turn and return to the imaginary center line rather than cutting straight through and dividing everything stiffly from left to right.

Remember, there is no mass of color to depend on for five to six months. But there are light and dark greens and stunning golden yellows in ligustrum and euonymus. There are accents, too. A handsome topiary of ligustrum, *Ilex crenata,* or *Photinia glabra* is as fine a detail on winter-gray days as statuary.

When a green garden is beautifully balanced, flower color is almost an intrusion instead of a necessity. A lovely green composition is complete and knows no season.

Time for Trees

November is the time to study trees, not when they are in full leaf. Now their individual outlines really show.

Total spread of branches, color and texture of bark, space at the top for sky room, basic shapes—all will be in sharp focus now. It is a fine time to learn that white oaks have beautiful pearl-gray layers of bark beginning about half way up, that dogwood branches are stacked in layers, that beech trees are ever more beautiful with their fringe of crisp brown leaves, that sourwoods keep their lovely fingers of dried flowers deep into the winter.

SOURWOOD

We can observe that hickory groups do well together because they grow slim and tall, while lindens need more room because they are round-headed. The black gums look like patterns in wrought iron, and sassafras is as fragile as flower stems.

If you have wanted a few more trees on the front lawn for a long, long time, have the enjoyable experience of choosing them right now. Drive in the country and look. Go to the mountains. By all means, go to a golf course on a foggy day and study tree silhouettes. Notice, too, how pines, cedars, and Cunninghamias warm up all other trees.

It is time to plant. Trees should become established slowly before being pushed by hot weather. Be sure they are comfortably grouped with existing material, leaving room for all.

There are fine books in libraries on tree identification, and nurseries have a good stock this time of year.

Native trees are always happy choices. Do not forget the silver bell tree, the native crab, deciduous and evergreen hollies, plums, maples, the white fringe tree, chinquapin, hawthorn, witch hazel, the cucumber tree *(Magnolia acuminata)*, and the black walnut.

Many homeowners care for and thoroughly enjoy beautiful, natural woodlands. You can add several more dogwoods, magnolias, and Cunninghamias over the years or simply let existing trees hold sway. Planting trees and caring for them in accord with your design plan is conservation in its truest sense and should be practiced by us all.

$\mathcal{F}$ALL $\mathcal{C}$HORES

SEPTEMBER: A month that gardeners have a tendency to overlook. August heat spills over into it, and no sooner does it get its balance than October slaps it down with a streak of chilly weather. If your plan is working out, and revisions and additions are not necessary, there are still a few basic concerns to attend to. Keep the soil worked and mulched, for hard soil will choke many a beautiful blooming plant. Add other perennials if desired.

OCTOBER: Do you remember singing "October's Bright Blue Weather" in grammar school? Use this month to your advantage, for there will be warm days followed by delightfully cool ones. New trees can be planted safely. Give yourself a Golden Rain tree (quick growth, deciduous) with beautiful yellow blooms, and a ginkgo tree (deciduous) with its stunning leaves of pure yellow in the fall. An evergreen gift to your plan could be a *Magnolia glauca* (sweet bay) or a hemlock, or both if space allows. They have totally different shapes and are two of the most beautiful evergreen trees available.

Take your plan to a well-stocked nursery and become acquainted with each shrub, tree, and vine. If you discover a new plant, do not buy several of them unless you are sure how big they will become and how much care they need. In fact, try to resist impulse purchases and experiment with new materials in your notebook before you acquire them.

Notice how other houses and entire lots look now. Look for a unified and attractive effect with no gaps in the design. The finer a house is in design and detail, the less plant material is required. You can always add, but it is a chore to dig up and discard. Some houses are not beautiful or well balanced, but many an ugly duckling has been transformed into a delightful and interesting composition by the careful use of high, medium, and low evergreen plant material. Concentrate on developing the eyes to see the problems and the patient planning to remedy them. A miracle is bound to happen.

NOVEMBER: Catch up on the dull chores first. Clean up all the dead leaves and remove all frozen and shriveled growth. Check all drainage. This is also a splendid time for necessary pruning, for no vine, shrub, or tree can hide a thing now.

Apply what you have learned throughout the year as you incorporate new ideas into your plan. If you do not have a handsome show of evergreen, you are exposed and have no place to hide. Make careful selections of trees and shrubs to add. Many an ugly new house or a sad, established old one has been turned into a wonderful, welcoming home because weaknesses were recognized and dealt with courageously.

If someone has dribbled a nightmare of cheap plants all the way around a house, remove the whole lot and begin with bare ground and the uncovered house foundation. Locate a group of three evergreen Carolina hemlocks on the left front corner and repeat with another group on the right front corner (these are your "high" groups). Between both corners and the front entrance, locate groups of three or five medium-tall boxwoods or three *Pieris floribunda* or, if in shade, three aucuba. On each side of the front steps, group three or five dwarf boxwoods, *Daphne odora,* or *Cotoneaster microphylla.*

Now you have high plants at the ends, medium in the middle, and low plants on each side of the entrance. To connect one group to the other across the front of the house, plant a strip of dwarf ivy. The result is entirely satisfying, with evergreen material that is balanced, in scale, and virtually maintenance free.

Epilogue

Your relationship with growing things can be very personal. Observe carefully how nature does its work.

If you want to have an unforgettable experience, choose and cut a stem of iris that has buds loosening up just a little. Put it in water and sit down beside it in a shady place or at late twilight. Then watch it open, even if it takes half the night. You will never forget hearing the outer petals make a rustling sound as they very carefully loosen and curve down. As this exquisite action is almost finished, the tall inner petals unfurl and straighten up, barely touching each other while giving a little sigh.

Your adventure with nature will continue in every season, all year long, year after year, for a lifetime. Let us go forward hand in hand.

cut a stem of
iris that has a bud
loosening up...

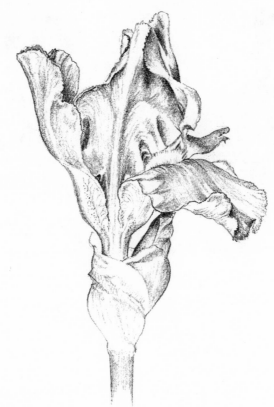

the outer petals
make a rustling sound
as they loosen and
curve down...

Purple Iris
Opened

Design Index

Plant Index